# INTO

# THE

# BEAR PIT

# INTO THE BEAR PIT

## CRAIG WHYTE

First published in 2020 by

ARENA SPORT
An imprint of Birlinn Limited
West Newington House
10 Newington Road
Edinburgh
EH9 1QS

www.arenasportbooks.co.uk

ISBN: 978-1-909715-64-6
eBook ISBN: 978-1-78885-103-9

British Library Cataloguing-in-Publication Data
A catalogue record for this book is available on request
from the British Library.

Designed and typeset by Polaris Publishing, Edinburgh

Printed in Great Britain by Bell and Bain, Glasgow

# CONTENTS

# PROLOGUE

IBROX, GLASGOW, 7 MAY, 2011

It was no use. We were stuck. There were fans everywhere, blocking the road.

'Let's just walk from here, shall we?' I said to the others in our taxi.

We stepped out into Edmiston Drive, gesturing to the guys in the taxi behind to do the same. Surrounding us were people clad in blue, white and red. Looming ahead, dominating the skyline to our left, was Ibrox Stadium, home of Rangers FC – the club which, as of yesterday afternoon, I owned.

It was my first visit to the ground since completing the takeover from David Murray. And it was match day. There were just three games to the end of the season. It was nip and tuck between Rangers and Celtic, as it always seemed to be, but three wins and the title was ours. Starting today, at home against Hearts in a lunchtime kick-off.

We'd only walked a few paces when people started to recognise me. You could hear a few murmurs. 'There he is'. 'That's Craig Whyte'. Then it started to build. Some fans started chanting. Many broke into applause. A few shook my hand and wanted their photo taken.

My first taste of what owning Rangers might mean had come just a couple of hours after signing the paperwork in David Murray's office in Edinburgh. My team and I had caught the train to Glasgow. It seemed the obvious way to travel between the cities, but seeing the new owner of Rangers on a busy commuter train was clearly surprising for some. By the time we arrived there were TV cameras waiting. That reception, however, was nothing compared to this.

As we walked towards the ground and the imposing structure of the Archibald Leitch-designed Bill Struth Main Stand – property that now belonged to me – we had a problem. How did we actually get in?

We asked a police officer. 'We'll get someone to escort you in,' came the reply.

The next thing we knew we were flanked by two mounted cops. We were now swept along on a wave of good feeling. The BBC reporter Chris McLaughlin caught up with me as we walked towards the ground. 'How does it feel,' he asked, 'to be walking inside Ibrox for the first time as owner?'

'Very exciting,' I replied. And it was. I could scarcely believe it was happening. To think a lad from Motherwell, who first went to see Rangers as a boy, could one day return to run the club. My dad, Tom, who in many ways was responsible for sparking my interest in both football and business, was among those accompanying me on this special day.

Asked about my priorities, both immediate and looking ahead, I told the reporter what my hopes were – that we would win that day and go on to win the league and that there were exciting times ahead.

As I reached the main entrance at the front of the stand, I turned and gave the assembled fans a wave. In response they gave a huge cheer. The sun was splitting the sky. It was a great day for football. In that moment it was impossible not to feel the overwhelmingly positive mood of the day.

Once I was inside the door, the chief executive, Martin Bain, was there to greet me. Given he had been one of the directors who didn't want my deal to go ahead, his presence here seemed charming. He shook my hand and asked if there was anything he could do for me.

'The first thing you can do is get that statement off the club's website,' I told him. Bain was a member of the independent board committee, a group set up apparently to safeguard the interests of the thousands of minority shareholders who made up 15 per cent of the total. No sooner had the ink dried on my deal with Murray than the committee put out a statement on the Rangers website saying they did not support the takeover and they didn't think the money was there to support the cashflow.

To say I was annoyed was an understatement. These guys were working for me now. I was going to have to put out my own statement saying what a load of nonsense it was and that some people had their own agendas – hardly the best start to a new regime.

The actions of that committee had been one of the reasons why, as the takeover edged toward completion, I had been considering walking away. I had never known a deal like this one. It was a big distraction. At one stage I'd instructed my lawyer, Gary Withey, to tell Murray's team that if it didn't go through quickly I was out.

It had been a lot of hassle, all this bullshit with self-important people thinking they had a say in things. Even at the last minute they had found ways to obstruct proceedings, delaying the original signatures the previous Thursday night. In the end I think it was David Murray who ordered Bain and the finance director, Donald McIntyre, to sign control over to me and my colleague, Phil Betts.

What none of us knew at the time was just how desperate David Murray was to get the deal over the line.

It wasn't the day for any unnecessary unpleasantness, however. Martin Bain left and the statement was taken down immediately. When he returned he joined my guests and I in the directors' room for a cup of tea before kick-off. He was pleasant enough. He told me there was a special seat for the owner of the club, and he showed me where it was.

We were civil to each other, but I think we both knew his days were numbered. The same would go for any other dissenters on the independent committee.

The match itself couldn't have gone better. Rangers were up against a depleted Hearts side, once again embroiled in speculation that the club's eccentric owner, Vladimir Romanov, was interfering in team selection. The Lithuania-based businessman had entered Scottish football with a bang but, despite some success, had made more enemies than friends. I hoped his experience wasn't a cautionary tale for the league's newest owner. Rangers comfortably won 4-0. The title was within touching distance.

After the match I held a press conference in the Blue Room. I wanted to carry on the positive feeling I had felt from the stands. The last thing I wanted to do was upset the team's title charge, so I talked of funds being available for new players and my belief that we could win the tax case which loomed ominously on the horizon. They weren't empty promises. At the time of the takeover I sincerely believed there wasn't a single problem facing the club that was insurmountable.

However, in most business deals of this nature, it's usual to be allowed access to the premises, to see what kind of company you are acquiring, to kick the tyres. That hadn't happened here.

It was only when the crowds had dispersed and the clamour about my arrival had died down that I got a chance to step out on to the pitch and survey my new surroundings. I thought of the times I'd sat in the stands – first in the Copland Road end and then in the Club Deck – watching David Murray's Rangers revolution take shape, the team's success mirroring my own upturn in fortune. My predecessor had brought elite foreign players to Rangers; he had reversed the club's policy by signing Catholics and had delivered nine-in-a-row. But what club had he left me? I still wasn't sure.

I thought also of the fans, whose rousing reception still rang in my ears.

Thanks to sections of the media, which had wrongly painted me as a billionaire, many of them no doubt believed I was going to invest heavily in their club. That was never the reality and I had never said as much. But as I looked around the stands I hoped would be filled with 50,000 joyous supporters in the seasons to come, I had an ominous feeling that my failure to be upfront about the challenges that lay ahead could come back to haunt me.

They didn't know the pressure I had been under from David Murray to spin as positive a line as possible: to praise his stewardship, to talk up the funds we might invest, to assure the fans that it was all going to be hunky-dory.

I had seen the expectation in the fans' eyes. Were these people going to end up disappointed? Transforming Rangers was my sole intention. But I felt they didn't appreciate what lay ahead. Perhaps I didn't either.

# ONE

FOR AS LONG as I can remember I was always thinking how I could make some money.

It goes back as far as primary school. While other kids my age were perhaps playing football or basic video games I was working out ways to get rich – as quickly as possible. It's not that I didn't try those other things. I gave playing football a try but fairly soon realised I was rubbish at it. I fleetingly wanted to be a pilot. However, ever since I was nine or ten I wanted to be an entrepreneur.

By the time I hit my teens the financial markets fascinated me. It was 1985 and I was 14 years old. The Big Bang revolution of the London finance industry was still a year away, but I was already planning my own first foray into a world that was opening up. I read up on the emerging traded options market. I realised there was a way that someone without money could make some quick cash.

Back in the pre-Internet eighties, BT operated an unsophisticated online computer service called Prestel – a precursor to the World Wide Web. I was still living at home, but in my room I had a financial markets screen very similar to what Reuters or Bloomberg produce today. I was a bit of an odd child!

Studying the markets, I spotted a trend in the shares of an engineering company called GKN. It was a bull market, so all share prices were rising, but GKN's were performing particularly well. I called up a stockbroker in Glasgow. It helped that my voice broke early and I sounded much older than I was. I gave my name and address and said I wanted to buy ten call option contracts of GKN for £2000. I knew the broker would send me a contract note and I had 14 days to pay. All I had to do was make sure I closed the contract before the 14 days were up. By the time I sold the shares they were worth £4700. I hadn't had to part with any money and they sent me a cheque for £2700. At 14, it felt as if I was a millionaire.

Those were the days before the regulation we have now. There was none of the nonsense anti-money laundering rules where you have to send copies of your passport and utility bills to confirm identification. I'm not sure there was even an age restriction. I didn't care.

What would I have done if it had all gone wrong? I would have been liable for the £2000 call option price. I didn't let on to my friends what I was doing. I don't think I even told my parents. I just started saving and continued trading. I didn't have a plan, other than to one day set up my own business. I might not have known then what I was going to do with my life, but I knew I wanted to be my own boss.

My parents both had their own businesses. My dad ran his company, Tom Whyte Plant Hire, first in Motherwell and then in Glasgow, while my mum Edna had a baby wear shop in the town's Brandon Street. We lived in North Lodge, considered one of the nicest areas in Motherwell. My younger sister Adelle and I enjoyed a comfortable middle-class upbringing. My parents came from working-class backgrounds but both embraced the freedom that came with being their own boss. They were also laid-back and liberal in their attitudes to life.

My sister and I attended the local primary school, Knowetop, but when it came to secondary school we had a say in where we wanted to go. Adelle chose the local state school but, largely because my friends were going there, I chose the private Kelvinside Academy in the west end of Glasgow.

Going there on the train gave me a greater sense of independence and freedom. It made me appreciate there was a wider world outside of Motherwell. It also had a bearing on my football preferences. Some Motherwell supporters might disagree, but many football fans in Lanarkshire have a local team they support and a bigger team they like to do well. It's especially true when the so-called smaller teams spend time in lower divisions, like Motherwell did in the early eighties. I had affection for Motherwell and used to go to games there with my dad from the age of eight. His company took hospitality at Fir Park and used to entertain some of the guys from Ravenscraig steelworks.

Rangers had always been in the background, but that changed when I started school in Glasgow – it seemed more fun and interesting to go to Ibrox than Fir Park. I bought a season ticket for the Copland Road Stand, the first to be redeveloped when the stadium was modernised. Rangers were not doing particularly well. It was the John Greig era, Aberdeen and Dundee United were challenging for the major honours and making great strides in Europe. The only decent player I can remember was Davie Cooper. There were days when he was worth the ticket price alone. The football might not always have been great, but the atmosphere was good. I was never a fanatical supporter, but I enjoyed going with friends. It wasn't the most important part of my life, but it was all quite enjoyable.

What wasn't enjoyable was school. I found Kelvinside uninspiring. My friends and I were pretty rebellious and if we didn't fancy going to school we would take the train through to Edinburgh and hang about there for the day instead. When I did go to school, I enjoyed economics and English. I had a head for arithmetic and numbers, but zoned out when it came to the more complicated stuff. That was my attitude with most subjects – what use would they be to me in the real world? What subjects did I need to know?

I didn't always get it right. I remember scoffing that I would never need to speak French and then years later I ended up living in Monaco and had to spend money on lessons.

Kelvinside was a rugby school, which didn't suit me because I was still interested in football. I was in the worst team, but we used to train on pitches that later would become Rangers' training ground at Auchenhowie, near Milngavie, East Dunbartonshire.

School annoyed me because even back then I hated regulations and discipline. At Kelvinside we were forced to join the cadets, whether it be the army, navy or air force. I joined the one I thought was the easiest – the navy. I thought it was all bullshit and gave the least effort possible, but every Thursday we were ordered to wear a navy uniform, complete with beret. Eventually I decided I wasn't doing it any more so I stopped wearing the uniform. The school still had the cane then so it was a bit of a risk to be so blatantly insubordinate, but at first nobody seemed to notice. Then somebody told me off for it and I was made to wear the navy uniform every day as punishment and march up and down the playground every night after school.

This was just before my 16th birthday. I had passed my eight o-grades and it was nearing the end of the term before Christmas. I told my dad I wasn't going back after the winter break. I wasn't having this any more. By that stage I had earned around £20,000 on the markets and probably had more money in my bank account than the teachers. My parents made a half-hearted attempt to talk me out of it. My dad made me pay the school fees that he was liable for. It amounted to around £2000, but it was worth it to get away. So, at 15, I left school for good.

At first I went to work for my dad. From an early age I had gone to the yard and washed the JCBs and other construction equipment. Getting to drive the big diggers at 13 was my idea of fun. Latterly I'd been helping out there after school and at weekends, when he paid me a fiver for two days' work.

When I first went full-time I worked as a hire controller. When people booked their orders to send the machines to the building sites I made sure they were there on time and the drivers knew where to go. I accompanied my dad to the building sites and learned so much there, meeting a whole host of weird and wonderful people. It was great experience. People wanted you to be efficient and they'd give you absolute hell if something went wrong. If equipment broke down, they let you know. If drivers didn't turn up or people showed up drunk, you had a problem on your hands. It was a baptism of fire, but I embraced it.

Once I had to find a guy who was missing from his shift. When I eventually tracked him down it transpired he had been in a brothel all night. The construction industry in Glasgow was a different world from the rarefied air of the City of London, where I would spend so much of my career, but the grounding I got there stood me in good stead for the challenges ahead.

I was working alongside an older colleague, but within months I became the more senior person. It was a dream scenario for a 16-year-old. I was still trading and I didn't have to go to school. I had more money than most of my friends, 95 per cent of whom went to university and were broke for the next three or four years.

I bought a motorbike – a pretty rubbish second hand one for a hundred quid – but I never sat my licence. Having driven the JCBs and 35-tonne trucks in the yard, I didn't feel the need to, and it got me about until I sat my driving test a few days after my 17th birthday. My first car was a secondhand black Ford Capri. With it came an even greater sense of freedom. Although I was working for my dad and trading, I was on the lookout for my next opportunity and, still 17, I set up my first business.

I started a company that rented mobile phones. The handsets back then cost more than £1000 – prohibitively expensive for most would-be users. But the coverage wasn't too bad and I could see the benefits for people using them on building sites. I gambled that by investing in a few of them I could make the money back by renting them out. I took an advert in *The Herald* advertising the service and rented them for £75-a-week, which sounds incredible given how cheap they are today, but I was satisfying a demand. In addition to construction firms, I rented them to BBC employees who found them useful for outside broadcasts.

I was spending the majority of my time in Glasgow, so the logical next step was to move out of my parents' house and into my own flat. I found one above the old fire station on Ingram Street, in the Merchant City, in Glasgow. The area was becoming gentrified, with a host of new builds springing up alongside conversions of older properties. Although I could afford the £500-a-month rent, my friends were students so our hangouts were the student union or places like Bonkers and Carnegie's. I had a few girlfriends around this time but nothing serious. Compared to my friends, who were mostly skint, I was probably a decent date, if only because I could treat them to meals in nice restaurants. My parents liked to eat out and my dad and I would often go for lunch, so I never felt out of place walking into more high-end establishments, even though I was still relatively young.

Throughout this time I continued to go to Ibrox. By now Graeme Souness had arrived and the transformation was instant. The signing of some top English players – due in large part to the lure of European football at a time when clubs south of the border were banned – was the injection of quality the Scottish game needed. When David Murray took over the club two years later they pushed on even further.

As the eighties drew to a close my dad sold his business to the BET Group, which became part of Rentokil. Initially we were both going to stay with the new owners, but very quickly we could see that wasn't going to work. First my dad fell out with them and he left. It was clear the company didn't want me around, so I swiftly followed him out of the door. It was the best thing that could have happened.

I decided to start my own plant hire company. I still had £20,000 to invest and the experience I had by this point meant I had a fully-formed business plan. I walked into the Bank of Scotland, presented my plan and walked out with a £60,000 overdraft. I then contacted several asset finance companies and set up a credit line to the tune of half-a-million pounds to buy the equipment to hire out. It didn't seem that outlandish at the time, as I'd been three years out of school, but looking back, it was pretty unusual.

I had to set it all up really quickly. It's not like today when many online businesses can be launched from a laptop. Starting a plant hire company was a serious undertaking. Once I had the funding in place, I found commercial premises by the famous Barras market in Gallowgate, bought £100,000 worth of plant equipment, set up phone lines, found my first customers, employed delivery drivers – everything. Whyte Hire was born. I was creating something out of nothing, but I knew the market well, I knew the equipment to buy and I knew the business. My dad had signed a non-compete agreement during his own buy-out deal so he couldn't work for me, but he was there if I needed his advice.

It was an exceptionally busy time, but it worked. In our first two years of trading we made a six-figure profit. I bought my first flat, in Lancefield Quay on the waterfront. I swapped the Capri for a Mercedes, then traded that in for a Jaguar XJS, before settling on a Mercedes SL with personalised number plates.

After the Club Deck opened at Ibrox in 1991 – the third tier of the main stand – my company took a box there. We would have a lunch before the game, some champagne and everybody got pissed. We'd bump into some of the players. Paul Gascoigne would come up and have a drink before the game sometimes, which I used to think was a strange thing for a footballer to do, but he was a character and nobody cared. They had a great team back in those days.

Things were looking up, but in our third year various factors conspired against me. The recession of the early nineties bit hard in Scotland. The construction industry is always among the first to feel the squeeze in any downturn and I was sitting with too much plant to hire. Then a major customer reneged on an outstanding bill, leaving me staring into the abyss. I sought help and asked one of the asset finance companies to restructure my debt. They refused. I was running out of options. I took advice from an insolvency practitioner called David Robb. He took me through the process. I set up a new company and put the old one into liquidation. Not one person lost their job. They all came with me to the new company. However, the pain of seeing a company go bust stung me. For a long time I didn't tell anyone, but in some ways that period defined my whole career. It was eye opening. I saw how things could be done and how ailing businesses could be restructured. The lesson was not to get too attached to one legal entity. You can restructure these things and keep going. That's what I did with the plant hire company.

Yes there were creditors that didn't get paid, but equally there were debtors who didn't pay me. It's the risk you take if you extend credit to someone. I accept that some people got hurt, but I tried everything to restructure the debt. You can either throw in the towel or look for a solution. If I had walked away from that business, everybody was out of a job. By setting up a new company, I saved those jobs. I believe that was the better way to go, but I can appreciate the criticisms. It was an easy decision to make. I wanted to keep the company going and it was a successful restructuring.

My new company became part of a wider Custom Group, a business services firm. One of the lessons I learned was to diversify into areas that didn't require such a heavy capital investment. I bought security companies, contracting businesses, cleaning companies, where customers could be found first and the staff hired after. The risk was lower. We did a lot of labour hire when the Royal Naval Armaments Depot at Coulport and the Naval Base at Faslane were being developed. I might not have made it as a cadet, but I could supply something to assist with the nation's defences. We had hundreds of guys working up there as part of that project. Soon the group was turning over £10 million and I was making £1 million a year.

I acquired businesses in England and started to look further afield, to New York and to Asia, where I travelled to Hong Kong, Thailand and Vietnam. Arriving in Vietnam, I was amazed to see there was next to no foreign investment. This was before the Asian boom and in Hanoi I found a city with over six million people, yet so unsophisticated. I'd arranged to meet a business contact there and, without an appointment, we went straight in to see the government ministers. I didn't go there with the intention of getting involved in anything in particular. I just went there to look for opportunities, but I ended up buying a factory that manufactured ceiling tiles. I also did a deal to send second-hand construction equipment over there.

I had enjoyed operating under the radar, quietly expanding my little empire, but eventually my activities were bound to get noticed and so it was in 1996, when a writer called Terry Houston approached me. He was compiling a book of *Young Scots In Business* and felt I was an ideal candidate. He interviewed me about my experience. I didn't see any harm in it, but a few months later the *Sunday Times* picked up on it and included me in its Rich List. It was my first taste of how journalists are able to twist facts to suit their own ends. It wouldn't be my last.

The *Daily Record* then jumped on the bandwagon and, amusingly, included me in a rundown of Scotland's most eligible young bachelors. I don't think they'd be so favourable today. They did me a favour when it came to meeting girls, but I was baffled by the press attention.

After the personal setback of the insolvency, my businesses were doing better than ever and my wealth increased. All I needed was someone to share it with. Although I'd had a few girlfriends, I hadn't met anyone I felt serious about. That changed when I was 25 and bumped into a girl I had first met as a teenager. Kim Martin worked for her family's steel business in Coatbridge and I used to see her and her dad when my father and I went out for lunch together. We were nodding acquaintances but got together after meeting in a Glasgow nightclub.

I was involved with a firm of stockbrokers and had met a couple of colourful characters who lived in Monaco. I didn't like paying tax – I still don't – and they convinced me the principality was a good place to live. I went down there and they showed me around. There was a lot to like, besides the tax benefits. It was warm and sunny and people seemed to enjoy more freedom there.

I found an apartment on Boulevard D'Italie, overlooking the sea. Kim came with me to Monaco. It was our first place together and it was an exciting time. I still had the Custom Group and commuted back to the UK from there. Before long, we moved to a new place on the seafront on Avenue Princesse Grace, where we had people like Philip Green, Shirley Bassey and Ringo Starr for neighbours.

It was another world out there. It was impossible not to be seduced by the glamorous lifestyle. In our first year there I chartered a yacht for the Grand Prix that May. I went 50-50 with a friend and we had it for a week, but when we turned up we realised it wasn't the best yacht in the harbour.

For the race, all yachts have to move five metres out from the harbour. We had a lot of friends on board for a party, but the bay was quite choppy that day. Some of our guests were feeling sick and wanted to get off, but they had to stay on board until the race ended.

I did toy with the idea of owning a yacht at one stage, but days like that, and the experiences of other friends who owned pleasure boats and private jets, convinced me it was better to short-lease or buy shares in them. The yachts might look amazing but even if you're a celebrity there's very little privacy because of the 30 staff needed to run them. Having said that, I have enjoyed many great days aboard other people's yachts and was always happy to get an invite.

Kim and I tied the knot in the gulf coast town of Naples in Florida, at the Ritz Carlton Hotel. We had been there on holiday and liked it so much we decided to get married there.

We wanted a low-key wedding, with little fuss and it was perfect.

As I looked forward to the new millennium I hoped it would be a time of new opportunities. But my next business setback was waiting around the corner. And the repercussions from it would be devastating.

# TWO

IN BUSINESS THERE are always things that go sour and there are always people who try to rip you off. When you acquire companies you hope you can turn them around, but it's not always possible. Any number of factors can turn against you. I've done a lot of turnarounds and by their nature they are messy. You take a firm through the insolvency process and sometimes creditors get left behind.

This was the case with Vital Security, a small Scottish firm I bought for just £120,000 in the nineties and merged into an English company. Although I financed the deal, I didn't actually run the company. The hope was that it could bring in contracts and improve its turnover, but it didn't work. The company stopped trading a few years later long before Her Majesty's Revenue and Customs (HMRC) came looking for unpaid VAT amounting to £200,000. The company had no value and was going bust, but I offered to pay the tax debt over a period of time. HMRC turned me down.

The case called at court in 2001. The cost of defending myself would have been £100,000. When I weighed up the consequences, it didn't seem worth defending. Technically, I was only a shareholder in the company, not a director. The person who was the director did turn up at court and basically laid all the blame at my door. He played the 'it was all Craig Whyte's fault' card long before it became popular. There was an element of truth in what he said, but he made it appear that I was a shadow director, acting behind the scenes, pulling the strings. The court accepted his explanation and I was disqualified as a director in the UK for seven years.

I didn't see the judgement as that big a deal. Like most government policies, the law on directorships ends up achieving the opposite of what it intended. Banning problem directors doesn't curb their activities. Anyone with half a brain can get around it, and it means the authorities can't monitor them.

The judgement was bullshit. It didn't affect me one iota. I was living in Monaco and by then had sold my business interests in the UK. The disqualification was due to run to 2009, but I shrugged it off and got on with life.

Kim and I were enjoying our time in Monaco. Our first daughter, Tiffany, had arrived in 2001 and life there suited us. It was good to see Rangers play there in the Champions League in 2000, when Dick Advocaat's side stunned the hosts by taking all three points in a group game. With a blend of foreign and homegrown talent, Rangers looked to have a team that could compete at the very highest level, but success in Europe continued to elude them.

I used to enjoy lavish lunches with a bank contact whose office overlooked the sea. Over one such meal he told me the bank's richest client lived in Costa Rica, a little-known tax haven which, he said, offered even greater financial freedom than Monaco. This was music to my ears. My view on tax is that transactions between people should be voluntary, and that goes for the government as well. Tax havens are completely moral as they stop governments from stealing your money. Governments are basically shakedown operations, like the mafia, but with better manners. They are parasites with no morals whatsoever. I was doing an increasing amount of business in the States as well as playing the American markets, and being based in Costa Rica would be perfect for the US time zones, as well as the tax situation.

I floated the idea to Kim as an adventure for our young family. She agreed, so I went hunting for a property. The house I bought was being sold by the American inventor of the boxes that keep pizzas warm. He'd sold his business for tens of millions, but renounced his US citizenship because he hated paying exorbitant taxes. I had some affinity with him.

At the same time we had a holiday house in Palm Beach, Florida, and I bought a house called La Tourilliere, near Cannes, in the Cote d'Azur, where 'Baby Doc' Jean-Claude Duvalier, ruthless dictator of Haiti, fled after being deposed in an uprising in 1986.

For two years we moved between houses, enjoying the rich variety these exotic locations offered. We celebrated the birth of a second daughter, Honor, in 2004, and relished our luxury nomadic existence.

I wasn't particularly itching to return to the UK, but two years on from Honor's birth I spotted an advert in *The Herald* that aroused my curiosity. Castle Grant, the 15th-Century former seat of Clan Grant, was up for sale. The 70-room house, in Grantown-on-Spey, in the Highlands, had been repossessed from its previous owner and I knew someone acting for the mortgage company. We went to have a look at it and fell in love with the location. It was beautiful, but the house was desperately in need of some tender loving care. It was almost a wreck, hence the distress sale, but that appealed to me. I bought it for £750,000 and it was exciting to be coming home to Scotland.

Once we moved in we realised the castle was completely impractical as a family home. It was the first time it had been used as such since the Second World War. We immediately set to work getting it refurbished, but the workmen were scared to go into the castle after dark. There were rumours it was haunted by several ghosts, including the sad spirit of Lady Barbara Grant, who apparently died of a broken heart after being imprisoned in a dark closet for falling in love with the wrong man. I didn't see or hear anything remotely spooky, but we heard from some of the workmen that tools had started by themselves. I was surprised by the number of people who were convinced the castle was haunted. We had guests who were sure they had seen and heard things. One of the ghosts was supposed to be a piper who had marched from Inverness to Castle Grant and piped around the building before dropping down dead. My mum came to stay and she was convinced she heard bagpipes in the middle of the night. One chamber in the castle was called the Skull Room and rumour had it the chief of Clan Grant killed the patriarch of the family that originally owned it and left his head there. If that was the case, it wasn't there when I bought it.

The castle wasn't the wisest investment I ever made but it was fun living there. Kim gave birth to our son, Lincoln, in 2008 and it felt our family was complete. The girls went to the local school and Kim got involved in the community. I'm sure the locals thought I was some strange guy who was hardly ever there. I had a flat in Belgravia, London, and spent weekdays there before flying up to Scotland for the weekend. My time was now spent acquiring financial services companies and trying to make them work. I bought several stockbrokers and asset management companies under the umbrella of Merchant House Group, of which I owned 30 per cent, and had an office overlooking St Paul's Cathedral. I was constantly on the lookout for restructuring opportunities. I owned diverse operations, from one that ran the buses in Surrey and Sussex, to construction companies.

By 2009 I had more than a billion pounds under management, status that would one day prompt the *Daily Record*'s unhelpful headline that this somehow made me a billionaire. There is a world of difference between being cash rich and managing other people's money.

I was working long hours and trying to juggle my business ventures with the responsibilities of a husband and father with a family up in Scotland. I thought I was pulling off the juggling act – but as far as my wife was concerned, I had failed. We'd always had a traditional relationship. She looked after the family, while I earned the crust. In her eyes though, I had abandoned her up there in our remote castle, while she was trying to deal with two girls and a baby. She wanted a husband and father who was present – and I couldn't satisfy her demands.

Matters came to a head on Boxing Day, 2009. Our marriage was broken beyond repair. I left the home and moved to London. Perhaps we might have been able to resolve matters had I not had a place to retreat to, but I felt I had no option but to leave. Within three months she took the children and moved out of the castle into a house nearby.

It took eight years to finalise the divorce. We had reached a settlement and after that I took the kids on holiday. While we were away, hundreds of thousands of pounds worth of items were removed from the castle. There is a lot still to be worked out, but I have been painted publicly as the villain. This is something I strongly refute. If I had to live my life again I would pay more attention to my family. However, it seemed impossible for me to spend time with my family and I was caught up in things I thought were exciting. I do regret not being there when the children were growing up, but it seemed impossible at the time.

After we split at the end of 2009 I had to adjust to life as a single man once again. To be honest, it wasn't that bad. I went on a few dates and tried to put the pain of our break-up behind me. I continued to travel to Scotland to see the children at weekends, but I threw myself even more into work. We were doing acquisitions on a fairly regular basis. Every day was full on. I was looking at deals, attending meetings about potential opportunities, managing businesses that we owned or were in the process of buying. On top of that, I'd have things to do in terms of the 20 companies I already owned. I had three different offices in the city, each with a fair number of people working in them. They all required different degrees of supervision. With some, if there was a good management team in place, my input was minimal, but if they needed a lot of attention it was very time consuming. It might have been a turnaround situation that I was managing very closely. In those cases any payment over £5000 needed my authorisation, so I was dealing with countless calls and email traffic. Almost every decision was coming back to me, but it was what I had spent my life doing and I could handle it.

However, it was against this backdrop that a unique opportunity came my way. Perhaps I was experiencing some sort of mid-life crisis. If I had been settled and happily married would I have entertained the notion of taking on another failing business – and one with a higher profile than anything I'd ever taken on before?

It was completely by chance that I bumped into George Cadbury, a member of the chocolate-making family, who had come in with a colleague to work on a venture for Merchant Capital, a subsidiary of my Merchant Group. George mentioned they were trying to finance a deal to take over a Scottish football club. 'Which football club is that?' I asked.

'Rangers.'

'How interesting,' I said. 'Tell me more.'

# THREE

THERE ARE MANY significant dates in the history of Rangers Football Club: May 24, 1972, the night the team beat Dynamo Moscow 3-2 to win the Cup Winners' Cup, and May 7, 1997, when the incredible record-equalling feat of nine-in-a-row league titles was clinched, stand out as glory days for the fans.

But another red-letter day is not commemorated, celebrated or acknowledged in any way. However, in some ways it is every bit as significant. On November 11, 1986, with the resignation of chairman John Paton, David Holmes took charge of the club. The move came less than a year after Lawrence Marlborough, of the house builders John Lawrence (Glasgow), had bought 29,000 shares from director Jack Gillespie, which meant that for the first time in Rangers' history one man had a controlling stake. Marlborough's decision to let Holmes, who had been the chief executive of the John Lawrence group, run the club was one of the most astute in the history of football in Scotland.

In 1986, Rangers were poor. Overtaken by Aberdeen and Dundee United, who were the dominant forces in the game, they were even playing second fiddle in Glasgow to a resurgent Celtic and had not won the league since 1978. Like many fans, I'd watched the team struggle on the pitch without really appreciating what manoeuvres were taking place behind the scenes. Before the mid-eighties in Scotland few fans cared – or even knew – who ran their clubs. All that mattered was what was happening on the field.

Two key factors allowed Holmes to transform the club. The modernisation of Ibrox – several years before the Taylor Report into the Hillsborough tragedy in 1989 forced every club to upgrade – and the ban of English clubs in Europe which enabled Holmes to lure Graeme Souness to Glasgow. The former Liverpool, and Scotland captain instantly reversed a trend of top talent departing the Scottish league. The signing of England stars such as Terry Butcher, Chris Woods and Graham Roberts helped Rangers win the league in 1987. A year later, when Marlborough, an absentee owner who was juggling the club with business interests in America, was looking to sell his shares, it was Souness who sold the idea of owning Rangers to his good friend David Murray, a businessman who had founded Murray International Metals.

At the time there was a danger Rangers might fall into the hands of the newspaper tycoon Robert Maxwell. Murray, who had previously tried to buy his boyhood favourites Ayr United, stepped in. Back then business deals could take place away from the prying eyes of the national media. By the time the press found out the deal was done, in November 1988, Murray was being unveiled as Rangers' new owner.

So began the nine-in-a-row league titles, first under Souness and then Walter Smith's management. Thanks to Murray and Souness and the signing of Maurice Johnston under the noses of Celtic, the club's unwritten policy of not signing Catholics that had stood for over a hundred years was ended for good. The bigger the names that came to Ibrox – Mark Hateley, Brian Laudrup and Paul Gascoigne – the more Murray's profile grew.

The fans were able to forgive the most foolhardy of signings as long as the team kept winning.

When Smith left as manager in 1998, Murray appointed the Dutchman Dick Advocaat and went for broke, almost literally. Advocaat's spending on players was like nothing seen before, setting a Scottish record with the signing of Tore Andre Flo from Chelsea for £12 million. Rangers' debts spiralled to £75 million. A share issue was launched to try to offset the impact, which Murray underwrote to £50 million, using money borrowed from Bank of Scotland, but it wasn't quite the success he had hoped for. Advocaat left in 2001 and, although Celtic came again under Martin O'Neill and despite a new culture of austerity, success continued to be delivered on the pitch thanks to Alex McLeish's last-day-of-the-season triumphs in 2003 and 2005.

But even back in the glory days of the nineties, not everyone was complimentary about the owner of Rangers. When the club laid on dinners for sponsors, I met Hugh Adam, a former director and the man whose millions raised through the Rangers Pools built the modern Ibrox. He told me he didn't think David Murray was a good businessman, which quite surprised me. I know there was a bit of history between them, but he was still a director of Rangers. Hugh Adam actually warned publicly as early as 2002 that Rangers faced bankruptcy. He was dismayed that the club had lost £80 million in five years and questioned how long the bank would keep financing the club.

I had only paid a little attention to the goings on at Ibrox in the years since I had left Scotland. In that time I don't think I went to a home match. I was aware Murray wanted to sell. In October 2009 it had been announced to the London Stock Exchange that Murray would consider selling his controlling stake. Since then I had read in the press about someone called Andrew Ellis trying to buy Rangers. It didn't cross my mind to pursue it until George Cadbury mentioned the club during the conversation we had, around June 2010.

The way George was speaking he seemed close to a deal. He had been speaking to Ellis and had the financing in place. 'We've almost got it done. We're financing it from the Middle East,' he said.

I shrugged. 'Well, if you need any help or input from me just let me know.'

That was that. I didn't hear anything else for a couple of weeks. I had no idea my colleagues were working with Andrew Ellis. Although Ellis was a contact of George Cadbury, he had no connection to the Merchant Group. I still wasn't that interested. Two weeks later I saw George again.

'What's happening with your football deal?' I asked him.

The financing had fallen through in the Middle East. Was I still interested?

'I might be,' I said, thinking maybe I could put something together myself. 'Why don't you introduce me to the guys doing to the deal and see if I can help take it forward?'

As I left George I thought it might be a fun thing to get involved with. Like I said, it must have been a mid-life crisis.

George invited me to meet Andrew Ellis at The Enterprise, a pub in Knightsbridge. Andrew's purpose for talking to me was to see if I was someone who could put money into his deal. I figured that was how George Cadbury had probably introduced me. We had a few drinks together and spent a couple of hours chatting. I enjoyed Andrew's company. He was quite entertaining and he knew about the football world. He'd previously been linked to a takeover of Queens Park Rangers and had led a consortium that paid £500,000 for troubled Northampton Town when it was facing liquidation.

Ellis was very keen on the Rangers deal. He had already met with David Murray a couple of times and they were in regular contact through text and phone calls. He told me he thought it was a brilliant opportunity, that he had the deal tied up but, crucially, he had no money. It sounds ridiculous but in business this happens all the time. You get the deal and then find the money. It's a bit like buying a house. You put an offer in before you've actually done the deal with the bank to lend you the money. The difference with Andrew's situation was that in most cases the person driving the deal has a bit of money behind them. He was still trying to raise the funds. He said it was his deal and he was confident he could get the money. From what I could gather, from speaking to him and other people, he didn't have any.

David Gilmour, who worked in Guernsey for a trust company that had administered an Employee Benefit Trust (EBT) scheme with Rangers, had suggested the deal to Ellis. Gilmour had wanted to be involved in the deal as well but he didn't have any money either, so they had been trying to raise finances in all sorts of places. Gilmour had approached Rangers cold about the takeover, but he and the club had this connection through the EBTs, a scheme used to encourage staff loyalty through bonuses and rewards. If EBTs weren't at the forefront of my mind at that stage, they very soon would be.

What became apparent was that in the summer of 2010, anyone with a chance of raising money was getting to sit down with David Murray. There was *such* desperation to sell. I now know they had a lot of bizarre approaches that weren't viable, but almost any half-credible business person could have progressed and got at least some basic information.

After speaking to Ellis, I thought it was potentially an exciting deal.

'I'm interested,' I told him. 'Send me some information and I'll see what I can do.'

I didn't commit at that stage – I never would on a first meeting. But I explained to him that I had a lot of contacts that I could potentially raise money from. I just didn't know whether they'd be interested in this. I also had a bit of money that I could put in, but at that time the asking price was £33 million and I wouldn't be able to cover the full amount. I didn't lead Ellis to believe I could write a cheque for that amount.

I enjoyed Ellis's company, but he didn't strike me as a particularly bright guy. He struck me as a football fan with big ambitions to do something but without the wherewithal to make it happen.

The Rangers project appealed to my vanity, and any business that gets nearly 50,000 regular customers who renew every year is one with potential. The fact that I'd been a supporter was less important than the prestige of the business, and my own knowledge of it.

Having said that, a football club was vastly different from any other business I had been involved in, and the last thing I wanted to do was move to Glasgow. I saw it as just another company that I could buy. I would put a management team in place to sort out the issues, maybe take it through an administration process if I had to. I didn't think the demands would be any greater than that. How wrong I was.

Back in the office the next day I saw my colleague Phil Betts, a specialist in asset finance. I said to Phil: 'We've got this potential deal. It's a football club with around £100 million in assets. Can you raise money on the back of the assets to buy the club?'

I was thinking of mortgaging the stadium or the training ground, a typical method of financing the purchase of a business.

Phil said he was sure he could. That's quite positive, I thought. When Phil says he can do something, he usually can.

He said: 'Let me make some calls and I'll come back to you.'

But a couple of days later he came back and said: 'I'm sorry. Nobody is interested in this. I can't do it.'

If he couldn't get the money that was it, as far as I was concerned. I wasn't going to start calling around anyone else. There would be no deal.

A couple of weeks on Phil and I met for a drink near our office.

'Are you still interested in that football deal?' he said.

'Yes,' I said. 'Can you get me the money?'

He mentioned a contact of his, Nigel Farr. Like I said, if you wanted something financed, Phil would try very hard to make it happen.

Phil said Nigel Farr had a contact that might help. Nigel couldn't tell Phil the name of the company his contact worked for, but Phil asked if I'd be prepared to meet them in a week's time. I was intrigued.

We met Nigel Farr in Paternoster Square, near St Paul's. He said the name of the company was Octopus Investments. This was interesting for two reasons. We knew Octopus was already involved with Rangers. The club had disclosed that to Andrew Ellis and David Gilmour. The investment company and fund managers owned Ticketus, a London-based limited liability partnership that had provided Rangers with working capital in exchange for future season ticket sales. Rangers had sold season tickets to them, about £5-6 million pound worth, over the previous two or three seasons.

The other interesting aspect about Octopus's involvement was that I had met their representatives about a year before, when they were looking for projects to invest in. Like a lot of people in the city they have vast sums of money coming in and they have to start investing it as quickly as they can. The last thing they want is to have money lying around not working when they are under pressure from investors to get a return. They had said to us to let them know if we came across anything we needed funding for, but I didn't think of them when the Rangers deal was first mentioned.

As soon as we heard Octopus were keen to back our deal, Phil and I asked if the company had a conflict of interest talking to us, given they were already dealing with the club. We were assured they didn't. I was a little surprised by this, but we took their assurance at face value and met Nigel's contact, Ross Bryan, who administered two funds for Octopus, Ticketus and Ticketus 2.

We got on well with Ross. He explained how the Ticketus model – one that was used a lot by clubs in England – worked. It allowed clubs to generate income at a time when cash flow is weak. Most clubs generate funds in the close season from season ticket sales, but once the season starts hardly any money comes in, apart from revenue generated by cup runs and European matches. By the time many get to January there's no money left. Selling future season tickets for millions of pounds sounds dramatic, but if you've got 40,000 season ticket holders, and the average price is £300, you'd expect to raise £12 million. Therefore, that club can raise £5 million by selling less than half of their season tickets for one season. That money still has to be repaid, however, usually over the course of several seasons.

It made sense to me. I had raised money to buy companies before using invoice financing, where you borrow money against the sales ledger, so this method was reasonably familiar.

We asked Bryan if Octopus would put up £10 million, through Ticketus. The purchase price was still £33 million. There was an equity element of £5 million to buy the shares. I was thinking I could raise that myself through various companies I controlled, and that there was a possibility that we could ask Lloyds Bank to continue to support the club, through the existing term loan, to the tune of £10 million. Andrew Ellis had advised me the bank would stay in.

Within 48 hours Octopus offered £10 million to assist with buying Rangers.

Now we were getting somewhere. We had a serious investor.

However, I started to wonder whether there was a way to take Lloyds out of the equation. Doing so would make it a much clearer deal.

'Do you think they'd do £20 million?' I asked Phil.

His reply was something along the lines of: 'No fucking chance, they'll never do that.'

He said he would ask them and before long he came back and said: 'You'll never believe this, but they will do it.'

'Well,' I thought, still a bit surprised. 'We're on.'

The Octopus fund managers were getting a lot of money in from Enterprise Investment Scheme investors, who demanded a better return than they would get in the bank. Octopus had to find a way to use that money so they could pay their investors a return.

Before committing, they wanted a personal guarantee from me and wanted a picture of my personal balance sheet. There was a process to go through. My net worth at the time was in the eight-figure range, but the majority of my wealth was tied up in private companies. I was still nowhere near a billionaire, as I'd soon be described, but I was fairly comfortably off.

Anyone in business will tell you it doesn't matter how much money they've got – what they want to do is use other people's money. That's how you get rich. I wanted to use as little as possible of my own money. We were going to pursue other asset finance options to cover the balance.

But we were a long way from finishing the job. This was still Ellis's deal, and I hadn't been back in touch with him since we'd met in the pub. I hadn't met the bank or David Murray. They could all have disappeared before things got serious.

We got a letter from Ticketus committing the funds, and that allowed my lawyer, Gary Withey, to tell Ellis's solicitors that we had the money for the deal. We had proof of funds, the credibility to talk to the vendor, to try to strike a deal.

Ellis couldn't have been more excited. He was like an overgrown kid with a Subbuteo set. He was beginning to dream of what it would be like to run his own football club.

I thought about how I would be able to manage those expectations. He was going to be disappointed.

This was my deal now. I told him to set up a meeting with David Murray.

# FOUR

LITTLE IN THE appearance of the man standing there to greet us suggested vast wealth or status. If David Murray was intending to set any kind of tone, it was very much informal. Dressed casually in a T-shirt and trousers, he seemed relaxed and happy to see us as we arrived at the door of his villa in Juan-Les-Pins on the Côte d'Azur. Only the crutches on which he was propped gave any indication of the struggles he'd overcome to achieve what he had in life.

If the evidence of the car crash that had robbed him of both legs when he was just 23 was the first thing to strike me, the next was the absence of any staff to help him. For any villa in the South of France, home help is a given, but Murray seemed to get by solely on the services of his trusted driver. That in itself was fairly remarkable.

He was Sir David Murray, of course, since being knighted for services to business, but as we shook hands I suspected he wasn't a guy for all the airs and graces that went with such a title.

I could tell Murray had Googled me because the first thing he said to me was: 'I see you own Castle Grant. I went there on honeymoon with my first wife.'

In those days my ownership of the castle was the only thing that came up on search engines. I wondered if that was all he knew about me. I was certain he hadn't heard of me before my interest was made known.

We did share some similarities. He was also young when he started in business – he was 23 when he set up Murray International Metals, turning over £2.1 million in his first year and making a profit of £100,000. Like me, he had studied a business-minded relative, in his case an uncle who ran his own scrap metal business. Unlike me, however, Murray seemed to enjoy playing sport, and had been returning from a rugby match when he suffered the crash that would end his playing days. That he was able to overcome that setback, not to mention the death of his first wife from cancer, said much about his character.

Two things had happened before we flew to the south of France in October 2010. Firstly, I'd agreed a deal with Andrew Ellis about how the takeover, if successful, would split between us. I said to Ellis that, providing he put up part of the money for the equity and any guarantee for the finances, I would be prepared to split the deal 75-25 in my favour. I would be the biggest shareholder. I doubted he would come up with anything. Ellis was just excited that the deal could be done. I think he saw that 25 per cent of something was better than 100 per cent of nothing, yet at that point he thought he was possibly going to be to running the club.

I imagined I would end up giving him something in the region of £50,000 – 100,000 for introducing the deal. That was what he was worth, but he had this fantasy about running a club. And it was key that I had our agreement in place before the meeting with Murray. If it was still Ellis's deal, there would have been no point for me.

As Ellis was the one in contact with Murray, he set up the

meeting. Before we left, I met Donald Muir, a long-time associate of the Rangers owner who was on the board of the club and of Murray's metal business. Muir said to me: 'David doesn't have as big a say as he used to because of the bank, but just go to France and tell him what he wants to hear.'

It was those words – and those of Hugh Adam, who had doubted Murray's business acumen – that were at the forefront of my thoughts when I finally met the Rangers' owner.

I knew Juan-Les-Pins well and had visited the homes of other people who lived there. Situated between Nice and Cannes, it is a popular spot for the jet set.

Our host was nothing but cordial when he showed us around his villa. It had views over the waterfront, but was more modest than I had expected, although I knew this was not Murray's primary residence – he had homes in Scotland, Jersey and elsewhere.

As was customary when buying a public company, a chaperone accompanied Andrew Ellis and I. In this case it was a lawyer called Rob from Murray's law firm, Dundas and Wilson. He accompanied the four of us to dinner – Andrew, David, his driver and me.

David was very hospitable, chatty and affable. His choice for dinner was a renowned fish restaurant, Tetou, near his house. It overlooked the beach where Napoleon had landed after his exile on Elba. Given how that story ended, perhaps I should have heeded the omens, but when it came to my own empire building I was very relaxed. If it happened, it happened.

David Murray, however, was keen to progress a deal. Over the course of the evening we didn't talk much about the business of football, we talked about business in general. David stressed the joys of owning a football club: how much fun it could be and how he had used it as a calling card for years.

I told him I was a former season ticket holder. That appealed to him, as did the idea of another Scottish owner. Everything was friendly. We got on well.

In these situations it is not the done thing to say where you are getting your money from, so I didn't mention it, nor did he ask. Murray didn't seem to be interested where the money was coming from. Why should he be?

We stayed the night at his house. Still there was no staff, which again struck me as surprising, particularly for someone with additional needs. I had staff in my house in France and everyone I knew had similar help. There was no appearance of anyone apart from his driver, who had come over from Scotland with him and came to dinner with us. Even that was a little bit strange.

Murray didn't surface for quite a long time the next morning, and when he did we only spoke to him for 10 minutes before departing. Nothing had been agreed, but as we left it was clear that both sides wanted to do a deal. We were both familiar with the next stage – his advisors would talk to my advisors to see if we could get it done.

I quickly discovered Murray's idea of due diligence. A week or so after my trip to France, Darrell King, a sports reporter for *The Herald* and *Evening Times*, called me. No journalists had my number, so I was surprised to get his call. How had he got my number? He knew I was negotiating to buy Rangers and he was writing a story, looking for a comment. I couldn't believe it. This was not how things were usually done in business.

Naively I asked if he would hold off for a couple of weeks. He said no. He brought up some business things from the dim and distant past. It was nothing embarrassing, just some detail about financial problems with a business I had bought years ago. I said I didn't think it was helpful for that to be mentioned at this stage and asked him to take it out of any article he was writing. He said he would. He emailed me the article he was going to write. I went through it: 'Can you take this out? Can you take that out?' He took it all out.

The *Daily Record* got in touch as well. I spoke to David Murray and said: 'How has this got out?'

He said: 'It's going to be in *The Sun* as well.'

It seemed clear that Murray had leaked it. Now that I know a little more about the way he operates, I suspect that was one of his ways of doing due diligence – get it into the papers and see if any shit comes back. If nothing negative came out, he'd go ahead. That appeared to be his *modus operandi*.

I said: 'I am not going to say anything now.'

My main concern was how so many journalists had got my number. Why were they calling me when nothing had really happened? I didn't want to speak to anyone. I certainly didn't want this in the press, because it might never happen.

I called Jack Irvine, a public relations executive I had known for a long time and founder of the Media House agency.

'Can you help out with this?'

'No,' he said, 'because I act for Rangers, but I can put you on to someone who can.'

The names he gave were Gordon Hay and Ian McKerron, two former newspaper hacks who had set up their own PR agency, Hay McKerron. I passed the journalists' calls to them.

Jack also said Murray had rung him up before our meeting to ask him how much he thought I was worth. Jack would have had no idea. From what I can gather, they agreed I was worth £80 million – I have no idea how they reached that figure and they certainly didn't ask me.

'David never calls me nowadays,' Jack said. 'But he called about you.'

Murray was obviously checking me out. The next morning I got text messages from friends saying, 'I see you're buying

Rangers.' I walked down to Victoria Station to see if I could buy a Scottish newspaper and picked up a *Daily Record*.

The front page screamed: 'BILLIONAIRE SCOT TO BUY RANGERS FOR £30m.'

What the hell?! Billionaire?! How had they come to that? I soon found out. In response to the enquiries from journalists, Ian McKerron had put together a small biography of me, and had said I had a billion under management. Clearly the *Record* hadn't understood there is a world of difference between assets under management and assets that you own. Maybe it was a reasonable mistake to make, but it wasn't true. In normal circumstances it's not the worst thing in the world for a single guy to be labelled a billionaire when you're dating women and they're Googling you, but this wasn't a normal situation. I found it mortifying. I thought it was potentially damaging to my credibility for a headline like that to be out there.

What I didn't fully appreciate was how it would look in the minds of fans. That initial description locked in a perception that I would never be able to live up to.

The piece by James Traynor – a name I'd soon be familiar with – said talks were at an 'advanced stage.' It went on to describe how I was 'a venture capitalist and business turn-around specialist' and that I was 'leading a consortium of other wealthy individuals.'

Incredibly it also said: 'If the deal goes ahead, Rangers boss Walter Smith will be given a massive sum to spend in the January transfer window.'

Where were they getting this from?

The *Scottish Sun* went further and said: 'RANGERS SOLD BY XMAS.'

On the same day, *The Herald* ran a front-page story: 'Rangers hold secret £30m takeover talks.' It said:

*LONDON-BASED millionaire financier Craig Whyte is in*

*talks to take control of Rangers in a deal worth more than £30 million.*

*The 39-year-old lifelong supporter of the team – who has made his money as a venture capitalist – has held weeks of secret talks with club owner and majority shareholder Sir David Murray.*

*The deal, which sources claim will be financed by Mr Whyte himself, would see Rangers' bankers, Lloyds, given about £25m to wipe out the club overdraft. It has been running Rangers under a strict business plan for the past year after stepping in when debts reached £32m.*

It went on to say that sources confirmed the deal was well advanced and that I had 'satisfied Sir David of [my] ability to take on the club, fund a deal and provide finance for new players in the future.'

As someone who had managed to successfully forge a career away from the spotlight, this was sudden, new and disturbing.

The *Record* noted that at 39 I was one year younger than the current Rangers' captain, David Weir.

The feeling across most newspapers was that this was great news for Rangers' fans. Also, there was a suggestion that news of the bid might force the hand of other interested parties. Rangers' director Dave King, a millionaire based in South Africa, had apparently tabled a bid, but it was deemed too low by Murray. However, King was embroiled in a dispute with the South African Revenue Service for unpaid tax it claimed amounted to more than £100 million and was facing 322 potential criminal charges. King had denied this and claimed he was the victim of a witch-hunt, but his assets were effectively frozen and I doubt he could have bought a car at that stage, let alone a football club.

Writing in the *Scottish Sun*, Bill Leckie suggested that any new investor in the club would surely be wise to avoid talk of deep pockets and endless funds for players and continue the recent belt-tightening at Ibrox. He went on:

*If the Whyte Knight is a smart cookie, he'll see all that and use his investment and business skills to improve on it. If he's a fool, he'll promise that the belt-tightening is over and it's time to large it all over again.*

*To be honest, I'm baffled by anyone who chooses to plough their hard-earned into such a perilous sport as this. As a wise man once said, the only way to make a small fortune out of football is to start with a large one.*

*But hey, maybe Craig Whyte WILL be different. Maybe he WILL succeed where so many others failed. Maybe, unlike his predecessor, he WILL make Rangers a club whose example every rival would be silly not to follow.*

Maybe I should have shut it down, and come out with a realistic appraisal of my personal financial position. However, this was all alien to me. My instinct, which had served me well throughout my career, was not to say anything on the record.

The leak had set the hares running. I did try to play down the speculation and sanctioned a statement to the Stock Exchange confirming my interest. It said simply: 'Mr Whyte confirms he is considering making an offer for Rangers FC and is in talks with Murray International Holdings Limited. But these are at an early stage and there can be no certainty an offer will ultimately be made.'

Whether it cut through the previous day's headlines was doubtful. The Rangers Supporters' Trust were quoted as hailing the talks as 'extremely positive'.

There were already mutterings from Dave King about whether the deal could be finalised and questioning how much money would be available. In an article in the *Record*, King mentioned that he'd spoken to Rangers' chief executive, Martin Bain, about 'statements made to the Stock Exchange'. It was perhaps the first sign of discord within the Rangers board. It would not be the last.

Once we had made the initial contact, I heard from David Murray on a regular basis. It was clear he was desperate for this deal to progress. At the same time, however, he warned me about Andrew Ellis's involvement. He asked me if I'd looked into him.

A nightclub-owner friend, James Mortimer, also mentioned to me that the fans didn't like Ellis. They apparently wouldn't back a deal with him involved. I wasn't sure what was driving that but I said to Andrew, 'Look just stay in the background and we'll sort it out.'

The writer in *The Sun* wasn't the only person who questioned my logic once the news came out. Some friends wondered what I was doing. When I appointed Gary Withey of law firm Collyer Bristow, I did so because he was a corporate lawyer with past experience of a football club deal. A mutual friend had recommended him to me. Gary had been company secretary and legal advisor to Crystal Palace when Mark Goldberg had bought it.

The first thing Gary said to me was: 'If you're buying a football club, you're mad.'

I laughed, but he was quite right. I should have listened to him.

# FIVE

PERHAPS MY PROBLEM was applying solid business logic to a football club. I was soon to discover this wasn't a logical business.

Here's how I saw it: we had a strong brand, with a loyal support, nearly 40,000 subscribers paying to watch the matches – guaranteed income. How many other businesses can claim that? If I could control the cost base I should be able to make a decent profit out of a football club. The trick, of course, is to keep winning, but in Scottish football the playing field is not level due to the size of the two Old Firm clubs, making success more likely. I could see a successful business model.

Where Rangers – and Celtic for that matter – struggled was trying to compete with bigger clubs in England and mainland Europe. In order to attract players good enough to succeed beyond Scotland, the additional revenue generated by European football was essential. Qualifying for the Champions League was worth around £20 million.

I believed if I could find a way to break even without having to rely on European football then I could make a success of Rangers. One of the ways to achieve that target was to look at every contract and find ways to improve them. As our discussions progressed, it became apparent that some of the variables Rangers had at the time didn't make sense. For instance, they didn't control the retail side of their own business. That needed to be rectified.

I saw Rangers as a medium-sized business with a couple of hundred employees. If it were an engineering company turning over £30 million, nobody would pay the slightest attention. It wouldn't have any clout at all. But because Rangers is a football club it gets massive amounts of attention and anything that comes out about it is front-page news.

I got a hint just how invasive the attention from the media might be when I returned to the Highlands a few days after the initial reports broke and was snapped in Aviemore. Even then, however, I didn't fully appreciate what I was getting myself into.

Another crucial element I didn't fully appreciate was the announcement from Walter Smith earlier that year that the current season would be his last as Rangers' manager. Smith had been a valuable servant to the club. He'd taken over the reins when Graeme Souness left to manage Liverpool in 1991, when there were just a few weeks of the season remaining. Rangers were in real danger of losing the league to Aberdeen that year and went into the final game against the Dons needing to win at Ibrox to win the title. They managed to do so and it set Walter off on a run to complete nine-in-a-row, equalling Celtic's long-standing record. Smith's final season, in 1998, ended without a trophy and he tried his luck down south with Everton. He provided much-needed stability when taking over from Berti Vogts as Scotland manager in 2004 and took the national team to the verge of qualifying for the 2006 World Cup. However, when Murray wanted Smith to return to Ibrox and rectify the damage done during Frenchman Paul

Le Guen's short but ill-fated time in charge, Walter angered large elements of the Tartan Army by apparently turning his back on his country.

The Rangers Smith rejoined was a very different club to the one he had left. Financial restrictions imposed by the bank in response to spiralling debts meant the manager could no longer splash out in the transfer market, as he had done before. Despite this, he pulled off something just short of a miracle when he guided the team to the final of the UEFA Cup in 2008, where they lost to Zenit St Petersburg. He won the league title in 2009 and 2010, before announcing that the end of the following season would be his last.

As that season reached the midway stage, Rangers were performing reasonably well and were on their way to winning a third league title in a row, although Celtic were mounting a serious challenge. Rangers had qualified for the Champions League group stages and although the team hadn't progressed in Europe's top tournament, it had made it through to the last 16 of the Europa League.

It was expected that Smith's assistant, and an Ibrox legend, Ally McCoist, would step into the hot seat. During the early negotiations I asked Murray what was happening on the managerial front, and what he thought of McCoist. He said said he'd spoken to Walter Smith and they all thought Derek McInnes would be a better manager. The former Rangers player was making a name for himself at St Johnstone after winning promotion to the top flight. David thought McInnes would be the best candidate for the job, but Martin Bain, the chief executive, had given McCoist such a ridiculous contract it basically meant it would cost too much to sack him, so it was accepted that he would succeed Smith. It was unfortunate not to have complete control over the managerial set-up but that was the situation I would be inheriting and when it was first explained I didn't see it as a major issue.

I didn't know McCoist at the time, and I was fairly optimistic about it. He had worked with one of the best in the business for years, and I didn't pretend to be an expert on football – I was willing to be guided by people. What was important to me was having a good relationship with the manager.

Murray was still extremely eager to progress things, and conscious of anyone who might cause problems. He was very annoyed with an anonymous blogger who had first broken the story of Rangers' financial difficulties with HMRC. I didn't know the blogger's name, but Murray sent me an email about him saying I needed to do something to stop this guy. I did think, 'Why did *you* not stop him?' A lot of the man's information seemed half correct but, while I had no idea where he was getting it from, some of the information looked to be of a specialist nature, containing specific tax details. The wider view in the public seemed to be this guy was right all the time, but a lot of what he was saying was wrong.

It was becoming apparent that Murray – and many Rangers officials and fans for that matter – thought everyone was against them. They really believed they were up against all manner of Celtic supporters working against them behind the scenes. I thought it was paranoia in the extreme.

However, one of the most significant revelations made by the blogger was that Rangers were facing a huge tax bill over the club's use of the Employment Benefit Scheme (EBT). This had all come to light before I got involved.

Use of EBTs began during the 2000/01 season. In the 13 years previously under Murray, Rangers had enjoyed a period of unparalleled success, winning 11 league titles and twelve cups. But as Sky's revolution of English football created a financial gulf between Scottish clubs and those in England's top division, Rangers began to struggle. The re-emergence of

Celtic also presented a fresh challenge on the domestic front. Although the bank had yet to start reining in the overdraft facilities, Murray was having to cut costs.

A former solicitor called Paul Baxendale Walker presented the option of an offshore tax arrangement whereby a company could place money into a trust, which was then split into sub-trusts in the name of nominated employees.

I'd actually met Baxendale Walker on a separate issue, completely unconnected to Rangers. He had written a book on remuneration trusts and wanted to talk to me about tax trusts. I met him in the Playboy club and we had a drink with some mutual contacts. He smoked a pipe and was very charismatic. He was trying to convince me he could make sure I never paid tax in the UK again and wouldn't have to live in Monaco. All I had to do was pay him £5 million. I didn't take him up on his offer.

The idea behind the EBT scheme was to reward loyalty through non-contractual bonuses and rewards. In Rangers' case, the recipients included 60 of the highest-paid players and senior executives, with the trusts administered by Murray International Holdings.

The EBTs allowed the company to make discretionary payments to the beneficiaries in the form of loans that did not have to be paid back. In such transactions neither the company nor the employee is liable for tax, because the payments from the sub-trust are supposed to be discretionary. There shouldn't be any contractual element in them. The club saved on National Insurance and they were able to attract players because they could give them more than if they had been paying them properly through the payroll.

It might have been considered a lawful scheme. However, everyone in the scheme was given a side letter by Rangers guaranteeing remuneration, thereby making it a contractual arrangement.

According to SPL rules, any player's eligibility to play for a club was conditional upon all documentation relating to their contracts and payments – including loans – being submitted. The side letters were not disclosed to the SPL.

From 2004, when HMRC became aware of the scheme's operation, its inspectors asked Rangers if such side contracts existed. Rangers denied that they did. When HMRC inspected the files, the letters were removed.

Their existence came to light after a City of London Police investigation into allegations of transfer irregularities involving Rangers, Portsmouth and Newcastle United in July 2007. In the process of that investigation, it seems police found something and alerted HMRC, who carried out their own investigation.

If it hadn't been for that police raid, the controversial nature of the tax case may never have been discovered.

The suggestion that Rangers might face a large tax bill first arose in May 2010, when the *News of the World* reported that the club might be forced to pay out up to £24 million for unpaid tax dating back over the previous decade.

When I raised the issue of the tax case with David Murray he made out that it wasn't a big deal. It had been blown out of all proportion. They were confident of winning the case and even if they didn't the liability was only going to be a couple of million pounds. We met with Murray's tax advisors. They were also quite bullish on the case. They believed it was winnable. Their view was that it was a legitimate tax avoidance scheme and a court would find in their favour. Even if the court ruled against the club, its advisors said the potential damage would only amount to between £2million and £5million. Andrew Thornhill QC, Murray's tax barrister, had apparently told him they had done nothing illegal and would definitely win any case.

I was fairly relaxed either way. Even if the club lost the tax case, the back-up plan would be administration. Either way we would emerge with a debt-free club.

What I didn't know at the time was that the existence of the side letters – revealed after years of suspicion and denial – hardened HMRC's attitude against the club. If I'd known any of this I would have taken a different view.

David Murray's attitude – or the spin he put on it – was that the inspector in charge of the HMRC account, Keith McCurrach, came from a long line of Celtic supporters. That was why he was going after Rangers. But that wasn't true. McCurrach just thought that Rangers hadn't followed the rules, and that the EBTs were a scam. He had the bit between his teeth, as we would soon find out.

Our negotiations with the Murray camp continued. Their side insisted on conference calls almost every day to keep things moving. I rarely participated in those calls. I left it to the professional advisors. I have never been involved in a deal where there was so much pressure on the part of the seller to complete. Normally it's the buyer putting the pressure on. I should have seen the warning signs, but I went along with it.

Another warning sign was Murray's refusal to offer any warranties. Normally when you do a deal you insist on all sorts of warranties as a safeguard if something goes wrong. If, on completion of the deal, you discover things aren't quite as they were described beforehand you can go back and claim on those warranties. But Murray refused to give any warranties with regard to the sale of Rangers. It was highly unusual. It is rare to buy a business without any warranties. Murray's argument was that Rangers was a company that was listed on the stock market with thousands of shareholders so he couldn't be held accountable – but he was the 85% owner. We asked for warranties but he vociferously argued against it and the deal proceeded without any.

Not everyone was keen for the deal to get over the line, however.

I would later learn that the majority of the Rangers board wanted Murray out, but the last thing they wanted was an outsider to assume control. I later formed the opinion that they wanted the club to fail, and my takeover to fail. I believe if they could have tipped it into insolvency they would have done so, if that meant they could buy it back and run it themselves. My arrival had disrupted those plans.

Stories had been appearing the media that were clearly designed to undermine me and the takeover. They seemed to come from an inside source.

Under the pretext of protecting the interests of the several thousand shareholders who made up 15 per cent of the total, the board set up an independent board committee (IBC) to consult on the takeover. The committee was made up of club chairman Alastair Johnston, chief executive Martin Bain, club legend John Greig, ex-chairman John McClelland and the finance director, Donald McIntyre.

The rest of the board was made up of Paul Murray and Dave King, who wanted to control the club themselves, along with Murray's men Donald Muir and Mike McGill.

The IBC had no power because the major shareholder had 85 per cent of the shares. Its role was to advise the shareholders whether to accept the offer or not.

I spoke a lot with Donald Muir. I considered him a decent guy. He encouraged me to meet with members of the board to hear their concerns. A meeting was arranged for me to sit down with Walter Smith, Martin Bain and Donald McIntyre, in the offices of Dundas and Wilson lawyers in Glasgow.

Donald Muir warned me beforehand not to trust them. He said to go and listen to them, be polite but don't believe everything they say. The way he described those guys was not very flattering. I had more of a relationship with Donald, so I was more inclined to believe him over the rest of the board.

To put it bluntly, they tried to put me off doing the deal. They were perfectly polite but made out there were a lot of problems. Walter Smith said there were only three players signed up for the start of the season. They said serious money needed to be spent on the playing side. They spoke about the tax case and cash flow difficulties. They were clear I shouldn't do this deal.

I spoke to Donald afterwards and told him what they said. 'It's not true,' he said. 'Don't listen to them.'

Maybe I should have listened to them. It was hard to know what to think. Everyone had their own agenda. The Murray side were desperate to sell. The club board were the opposite.

What surprised me was how disrespectful they were about David Murray. They didn't seem to hold him in very high esteem. They almost treated him like a joke figure. The Murray side and the non-Murray board members were basically at war with each other. They hated each other. I was caught in the middle.

I found Martin Bain perfectly amenable in these early meetings but there had been suggestions from some quarters that he couldn't be trusted.

I met Alastair Johnston one-on-one in the offices of Dundas and Wilson. He said something about, 'all this publicity, all this fuss over this wee football club'. At the time I was shocked to hear the chairman referring to the club like that. He was working with IMG in America and I was to discover he was absolutely right. In global terms, the business is small.

Amid this conflict, it was hard for us to get access to relevant information. The club tried to block us seeing any kind of documents. We were also concerned about Murray's side not disclosing documents and we considered there was a lot of information missing from the data room, the facility by which information can be passed between both sides.

Murray could have asked us at any point to clarify our source of funds. We had made it clear we were using third-party funds to finance the deal. If Murray or his advisors were unclear about that they could have asked, and they didn't. They didn't care.

As the weeks rolled into months and we headed into spring 2011, the pressure on us to conclude the deal intensified. I didn't know it then but for Murray the clock was ticking.

And as we neared the finish line, some serious red flags were about to be revealed.

# SIX

I MET DAVID MURRAY on three more occasions – at his house in Perth and his offices in Charlotte Square, Edinburgh. The meetings were informal and friendly. They were opportunities for us to get to know each other, away from the advisors.

I thought we got on extremely well. David opened up about his own company. The Bank of Scotland was effectively liquidating Murray International Holdings (MIH). It wasn't a formal liquidation and the bank was paying Murray to handle it. He spoke about restructuring his business. He wanted to get his businesses away from the bank-controlled MIH into a new private company that he had with his sons. It sounded noble.

We had a lot in common in the way we spoke about buying businesses and restructuring. He financed acquisitions using the same methods as I did, yet only a year later he would claim to have been shocked to learn that my takeover was third-party funded.

What I didn't know was that the Bank of Scotland had given Murray a deadline by which time he had to have sold Rangers – or he wouldn't be able to take back ownership of his metals business. For David Murray, the sale of Rangers had to go ahead.

The closer we neared to that deadline – one I was completely in the dark about – the more intense the pressure from the Murray team became. Donald Muir was advising me constantly on how to play Murray and how to play the independent board committee. Again, there were things I didn't know about his own motivations. He was highly conflicted.

In early April 2011 we were still pushing for full disclosure of documents into the data room. Eventually, things started coming out of the woodwork. The Murray team revealed what would become known as the 'small tax case' liability. This was another tax avoidance scheme the club had been running. The discounted option scheme was another Baxendale Walker had advised them on. To this day I'm still not sure exactly how it worked, but it was a device to avoid paying PAYE income tax and national insurance. It was a different scheme set up separately to the EBTs for only three players. The potential liability, however, was £2.8 million. At that time this was still around the level they were telling us we might have to stump up for the 'big tax case'.

We then found out that the stadium wouldn't be allowed to open for the 2011/12 season unless a new public address system was installed and the catering facilities were upgraded. This would cost another £1.7 million.

These were huge red flags. I should have delayed things, asked to investigate further. We did protest about these late disclosures but the Murray camp, so desperate to keep things moving, responded by reducing the purchase price from £5 million to a pound. Again that should have been a major sign that there were other issues to be revealed; they were so desperate to get rid of it they were giving it away for nothing.

However, by then I had the Ticketus financing in place and my thinking was that the deal had just got better. I had pulled together about £4 million from some funds I had under management and a pension fund, but this development meant I didn't have to rely on that. The deal was going to be simply about debt financing. There was so much pressure from the Murray side to get the deal done, with these nightly conference calls and daily calls from Donald Muir and McGill. I could have stopped it but it was going to be difficult to walk away at that stage. With so much momentum behind it, I knew by then the deal was going to happen.

As we neared towards completion I thought the situation actually suited me quite well. Administration seemed almost inevitable, so any money that would have been paid out would have been wasted. I felt it was moving in my direction.

I consulted my team, which by then included financial advisors at a firm called MCR, a corporate restructuring and turnaround firm focused on insolvency administration that had offices in London, Manchester and Birmingham. Phil Betts had introduced me to David Grier, a specialist in rescuing failing businesses. We had met for the first time a year or so before. David was sure he could help me renegotiate the debt Rangers had with Lloyds Bank. I gave him a performance-based deal – if he got the debt with Lloyds reduced significantly, he'd get a fee.

MCR hadn't had any prior dealings with Rangers. We had the £20 million from Ticketus, so if MCR could get the debt down from £20 million to £10 million we'd still have £10 million in reserve. I consulted closely with David Grier at MCR and soon would consider him a friend. I had very little dealings with his fellow partners Paul Clark and David Whitehouse at that stage.

On the share purchase agreement with the Murray team we had mentioned the potential of insolvency events and administration. Now the price had come down to a pound, we looked at the possibility of putting the club into administration pre-acquisition, or at the time of the takeover.

We decided Murray wouldn't agree to a pre-acquisition administration because he was clearly concerned about his legacy, but we discussed a pre-packed administration on day one. I discussed this with my legal team, with Octopus and with MCR. It looked like a less risky way of doing the deal.

All of the problems would have been parked, from a public relations perspective, with the old management, and we would start with a clean slate. We would have got rid of all the debt on day one, with no impact on me.

The argument against this, though, was that we expected to hear the outcome of the EBT tax case within the first month of the takeover. The hearing was supposed to take place the week before acquisition, but it was put back a month. If we put the club into administration and then found we'd won the case, that wouldn't look great.

Although I felt the deal was moving in my favour, the insistence of Donald Muir and Mike McGill for me to meet with the independent board committee once more tried my patience. The deal was already a huge distraction, taking up far more of my time than I ever anticipated. I was beginning to wonder if it was all worth it. I said to Gary Withey to tell them, 'If this doesn't get through quickly, I'm out.'

It was too much hassle. Why was I having to meet all these people? With other business deals, you don't get all this bullshit with independent committees and self-important people thinking they have a say in things.

I didn't want to meet them at all. It was a pointless exercise. Of the 24,000 punters that own 15 per cent of the remaining shares, most of them retain them for souvenir value. I thought the board were a bunch of pompous buffoons and meeting them served no purpose. I didn't need them. I said all this to McGill and Muir: 'I don't really want to meet these people. There's no point. They can't block the deal. They can't do anything. Why do I have to waste my time going to see these people?'

Mike McGill said: 'Please, will you do it? It makes my life easier if you go up there.'

Eventually, as a favour to Muir and McGill I agreed. I wanted as smooth a transition was possible, so I went along with it. It was the middle of April and we were very close to completion. Around that time I went to a Rangers match against Celtic. Donald Muir told me he much preferred the Celtic directors to the Rangers board. They were a much better bunch of guys, apparently. A meeting was arranged at Rangers' training ground at Auchenhowie.

Joining me were Gary Withey and David Grier. For Rangers I think there were Martin Bain, Donald McIntyre, John McClelland, John Greig and Alastair Johnston.

By that stage they knew the deal was close to going through. There were more questions about potential working capital and so on for the business going forward. I told them that by our projections we needed to be in the Europa League at worst. If we managed that then the working capital would be fine.

They were trying to dig into my personal wealth and background. They didn't quite go as far to say how much money do you have, but that's what they were getting at.

I said the money was there to do the deal, that was all they needed to know. We had given proof of funds and anything else relating to me was irrelevant. I had already decided they were all going to have to go sooner rather than later, but I underestimated the bad feeling within this group, and failed to see their agenda.

I insisted that as part of the deal there would be a sub-committee of the board comprising of my colleague Phil Betts and I. We would have full executive authority – we wouldn't have to consult the rest of the board. We believed then that if we had just left it to the directors we wouldn't be able to do anything. As it was, the actions of some of them hamstrung us anyway.

I set up a new company, Wavetower, specifically as an acquisition vehicle for the takeover of Rangers FC. I had a holding company called Liberty Capital, registered in the British Virgin Islands. It owned a lot of my investments. It seemed the obvious place to park Wavetower. Although I was no longer having to put up my own money, both entities provided the personal guarantee with Ticketus. Effectively though, it was Rangers giving the guarantee. Although Ticketus owned the season tickets, I naively thought that as long as there was a team called Rangers, playing at Ibrox, my guarantee was safe. I just had to make sure Rangers continued to perform.

I could only be held liable for whatever wealth I held in my name. Any other business of value that wasn't owned directly by me or by Liberty Capital was unaffected.

The deal was due to be concluded in the offices of Dundas and Wilson in Edinburgh on Thursday, 5 May 2011. We assembled in a large conference room. All the legal teams were there, as well as a representative from Lloyds Bank. Everybody was keen to drive it on and get the deal done. Everyone, that is, except Martin Bain and Donald McIntyre. They went missing. Everyone was waiting and they were needed to sign forms to enable us to control the club's bank account, and so the independent committee could give full control to Phil Betts and me. We stayed late on Thursday, but their intransigence meant the takeover could not happen that day. The atmosphere was incredibly tense.

Phil and I stayed in a hotel while David Murray convinced Bain and McIntyre they had no choice but to sign these forms. I'm sure his metals business was at the forefront of his mind.

Murray sent an email to Bain and McIntyre in which he said they had to do this deal. He said there's no other option, things are going to be very bleak if this deal doesn't go through.

It's hard to say what would have happened to Rangers if I had walked away at that moment. The bank may have continued to support the club just because it was the easiest option, but they would have continued reducing its facilities until the outcome of the HMRC case.

By the following day we had everything we needed and the takeover finally completed. Someone flicked a symbolic pound coin across the table as we signed the deal.

I was the new owner of Rangers Football Club.

The solicitors had a little champagne reception in the office. A few bottles of bubbly were opened and there was a toast of congratulations. It was all quite low key – a mixture of relief and elation after all the obstacles we'd had to overcome. Given the tension of the previous 48 hours it was amazing we had actually got it over the line. I had to pinch myself while the ink dried. Was this really happening?

I'd already had a taste of how David Murray's relationship with the newspapers worked. Within five minutes of signing the deal I got another. We were alone in the office. He picked up his phone and dialled a number. 'I want you to speak to a friend of mine.'

He handed me the phone. At the other end was Bruce Waddell, editor of the *Daily Record*. Okay, I thought. The whole media relationship thing was clearly extremely important to David. I had a brief chat with Waddell. He offered congratulations. There was mention of meeting up once I'd had a chance to get settled.

Murray was keen to put out a press statement. If it had been solely up to me this would have been the moment to temper expectations, but Murray was eager for me to say how we were going to be investing in the squad; for me to praise his stewardship of the club; to reassure the fans that the future of their club was secure.

My statement said:

*The guiding principle from the outset has been to get the right deal for Rangers. I know the time this has taken has created a lot of frustration, but it was vital we secured a deal that meant we could maximise investment in the team and that is what has been achieved. As a keen Rangers supporter I now look forward to helping the club secure its future as a leading force in Scottish and European football. I know the club has gone through some difficult spells in recent times but it is my commitment to the manager, his backroom team, the players and, most importantly, the loyal supporters that I will do all I can to ensure further success in the weeks, months and years to come. Rangers is a great club with a great future. It has the best supporters in the world and I will do everything possible to protect and enhance the club's standing going forward.*

*I would like to personally thank Sir David Murray for the way in which he has conducted his side of this difficult and complex negotiation, as well as for the devoted service he has given to Rangers over many years. His is a great legacy of which he can be proud. Now the really hard work begins and I would appeal to everyone who has the best interests of Rangers at heart – the management, the players and the fans – to give the club the support it so richly deserves.*

My team and I left the offices and caught a train to Glasgow. By the time we arrived, television cameras were at Queen Street station.

I had my first sign of what like would be like as the owner of Rangers.

I was going to be living in a goldfish bowl. It felt momentous and I felt very privileged to be in this position, but was I really ready for this? No sooner had we got to the Hilton when the first challenge presented itself.

Gordon Hay and Ian McKerron had been getting calls from the media. The independent committee statement had gone live on the club website. It said:

*Although the IBC has no power to block the transaction, following its enquiries the IBC and Wavetower have differing views on the future revenue generation and cash requirements of the club and the IBC is concerned about a lack of clarity on how future cash requirements would be met, particularly any liability arising from the outstanding HMRC case.*

Alastair Johnston had announced his intention to resign as chairman on May 16. He hinted that sceptics on the IBC would have their say about my stewardship further down the line. I vowed to make sure they would not do so as active members of the Rangers board. We had dinner at the Hilton and in the morning my dad joined me, as well as Hay and McKerron, as we jumped in the taxis to take us to Ibrox.

Those scenes in Edmiston Drive before the game will live with me forever. Being cheered into Ibrox and sitting in the owner's seat were surreal experiences. Having my dad there to share it was extra special. I hadn't had a chance to speak to Ally McCoist before that day's game, but the team performed well and although Walter Smith was stepping down, there were reasons to be optimistic.

The priority was not to do anything that distracted from the team. Win three games and we'd be champions. But even walking around the stadium that day, I could see many things that needed to be addressed. The toilets hadn't been touched for years and there was work to be done before Ibrox could even be deemed suitable for the next season.

In my post-match briefing with the press I mentioned tackling the sectarian issue. Rangers had been punished by UEFA for singing unacceptable songs and our fans would be banned for the next European away game. I hoped the consequences from that wouldn't be too damaging.

After six months of intense negotiating we had finally done it. I was the owner of the biggest, most successful club in Scotland, one of the most prestigious in Britain and one that I hoped could be a force in Europe. The task was daunting. The hard work was only just beginning.

# SEVEN

WHEN YOU TAKE over a football club it's a bit like the birth of your first child. You look at it and think, 'What do I do with this?'

I went in thinking I could treat it like any other business – go in, cut costs, make tough decisions. That proved to be a big mistake. With a football club you have to be more like the leader of a political party than a businessman. You've got the supporters, who are your constituents. You've got to try to keep them happy. You have the press following your every move, like the political lobby. You've got to feed them constantly or else they'll start digging around for their own stories. At the same time you have to make proper business decisions. It was a weird set-up for anyone not used to it and I was plunged right into the deep end. In other circumstances I might have had a couple of years to find my feet. In that time, any mistakes would not be critical. At Rangers there were no second chances.

I was now a public figure and getting recognised everywhere I went was bizarre, not to mention being snapped by photographers outside One Devonshire Gardens, the hotel I'd elected to stay in while in Glasgow. Everywhere I went I had people shaking my hand and beeping their car horns. It was surreal.

One of my first tasks was an interview with Rangers TV – my first chance to tell the fans how overawed I'd felt at the reception I'd received the previous Saturday. I did the obligatory pose with the Rangers scarf above my head. I said I was confident we would win the tax case – the advice at the time continued to be positive. I hoped to speak to Ally McCoist that week, I said, to discuss players' contracts and potential signing targets. The team had a must-win match against Dundee United on Tuesday night, so again my priority was not to say or do anything that upset those preparations. Lee McCulloch was quoted after the Hearts game saying the takeover had given everyone a lift. I hoped that feeling would continue when we were back at Ibrox for the penultimate game of the season. Dundee United made it difficult, but goals from Nikica Jelavić and Kyle Lafferty put us four points clear with one game to go. Celtic were playing the following night, but win our last match away to Kilmarnock and the title would be ours. As much as the match was about getting one hand on the trophy, the night really belonged to Walter Smith – as it was to be his last as manager in front of the home fans. The reception he received befitted the service he'd given the club, the crowd, almost to a man, staying behind to send him off.

Off the park, there was so much to get on top of. The club's main offices are in Argyle House on the other side of the main stand. It was a rabbit warren and not a particularly great working environment. A lot of the first week was spent with the advisors, planning the finances for the new season. I spoke to the marketing team about promotions for season tickets. I was learning about a business I'd never worked in before, so I wanted to meet the people and try to assess what needed to be done.

One of the most pressing things was the state of Ibrox. I knew there was some urgent health-and-safety work to be done. The takeover contract specified that £1.7 million had to be spent on the PA system and the fast food outlets, and if that work hadn't been done by the start of the season Ibrox wouldn't open. We would have to find another stadium to play in. That's what I knew about. What I didn't know about was other work – some of it very expensive – that had to be carried out on the roof. As soon as we went in we were hit with all these things. I couldn't say yes to everything, I had to make an assessment of what was urgent from a health and safety point of view and what we would like to get done in an ideal world. There were significant amounts of money spent on the stadium. It was built in the 1970s and not a lot of work had been done since then. It needed a complete overhaul.

I had a brief meeting with Ally McCoist during that first week, but only to say that we would sit down once the season was over.

That last day of the season will always stay with me. On the way to Kilmarnock and before kick-off I was nervous. I feared it might come down to an anxious last few minutes, with one ear on the Celtic score. I needn't have worried. The team were superb. Any fears or nerves were blown away when we raced into a three-goal lead inside the first few minutes. Rangers ran out 5-1 winners and although Celtic also finished strongly we clinched the title by a point. Rugby Park was packed with Rangers fans and after the trophy presentation we headed back up the road to Ibrox for a party as 40,000 supporters celebrated a world record 54th league title.

The reception was incredible. Dozens of boisterous fans mobbed me outside Ibrox. I needed the police to get me into the ground. On the pitch I watched as the players and management that had made it happen got their hands on the league trophy. I even got a chance to hold it aloft. Never in my wildest dreams did I ever think that would ever be a possibility when I started going to watch Rangers back in the eighties.

Seeing the smiles on everyone's faces, the joy another title meant to people, gave me a brilliant feeling. For one fleeting moment all the negativity that had surrounded the deal – the tax case, the board members with their own agendas, the bank debt, the crumbling state of Ibrox – disappeared. I looked around the packed stands and imagined more days like this in the years to come.

After the match Martin Bain said, 'I really want to work with you, Craig. Let's make this work.'

I had an open mind on working with him. When you take over a business you want to bring in your own people, but with Martin Bain there was a possibility I could keep him on.

Sadly, that was the best it would ever be.

From that day on, anything that could go wrong did.

For a brief spell I thought I could control the negativity.

Not long after the takeover, a sports reporter for the *Daily Record* wanted to reveal Ticketus as the source of our third-party funds. I got the story pulled.

At the time, it seemed the only move to make. For a start there was a confidentiality agreement in place with the fund managers, which was fairly normal in a commercial situation. After all, Rangers had kept their own previous arrangement with Ticketus confidential.

There was definitely a belief inside Ibrox that the club was special. Martin Bain said to me early on that we always needed to give that impression to the fans. He had been there a long time and wasn't taken in by the whole thing, but he used the expression, 'We've got to keep up the smoke-and-mirrors act. We are Rangers. We are this big club. Never let up on that.'

When I saw how certain sections of the media could bend to your will I began to see he had a point.

That was also part of my mindset when it came to the Ticketus deal. I had the fans to think about. Might they be upset at this type of financing being used? In fact I'm not sure anyone cared that much, but that was the thinking at the time – the fans might not like it. The big worry for any football club is that the supporters boycott buying season tickets. That would be a major problem. Fans of football clubs have more power than they think. If they boycott season tickets any club is screwed, so they'll do whatever the fans want them to do.

The Ticketus story was coming to light in the period when we were trying to get the season ticket money in. We didn't want anything to jeopardise that. With hindsight, we should have been upfront about it.

I still didn't view it as remotely controversial. It was a method of financing at around 10 English Premier League clubs, although it was largely kept quiet. A watered-down story appeared, questioning whether future season ticket sales would be used, likening it to a scenario that had led to Leeds United and Newcastle United getting into financial difficulty. However, a subsequent story in the *Scottish Sun* assured fans that wasn't the case.

It seemed the wrong time for that to come out. I had enough on my plate. I was more interested in getting the board under control and making sure the stadium could open its doors next season.

I had the issue of our fans and the sectarian element that had blighted the club's reputation. UEFA had come down hard after offensive songs had been sung at both legs of a Europa League tie with PSV Eindhoven in March. At one stage there was the awful spectre of Ibrox being closed to supporters for two games. In the end the punishment was severe enough –

a £35,000 fine and a ban on Rangers fans travelling to one European match, with further home and away bans suspended for a period of three years. Martin Bain had called the action a 'deliberate and targeted campaign' – something I would hear a lot when it came to anyone who challenged the Rangers way – but it was still a problem I wanted to get on top of. My first taste of matches at Ibrox had been very encouraging. There hadn't been any sectarian singing. I was extremely keen for Ibrox to become a place where families could come and fans could enjoy themselves without bigotry.

The recent Scottish Parliament elections had returned the SNP government with an overall majority and already there were noises out of Holyrood that ministers wanted to crack down on offensive behaviour. The fans had to realise that times had changed and any punishments, financial or otherwise, would seriously hurt the team.

One thing I didn't expect to have to deal with was having David Murray still calling me regularly. More often than not it was about some small issue – something in the papers, or something Martin Bain had said to him. I had been in to see the chief executive in his office, but Murray would tell me Bain thought I wasn't talking to him. Murray was concerned to hear this. It was soon to be a common occurrence. Often he would call me at the most inopportune moments, like Sunday evenings. He didn't always want to talk about football, just whatever was going on in his life. He had announced he was getting married again. It was a new chapter for him. Was he finding leaving his old life harder than he anticipated? It was certainly unusual. Normally in business when the deal's done that's it – the previous owner is gone. You don't talk to them.

Alastair Johnston would soon be vacating the role of chairman and I would assume the position. Part of the rigmarole I had to go through was to satisfy a 'fit and proper person' test for the

Scottish Football Association (SFA). It had been introduced for owners of all British football clubs since 2004, aimed at preventing corrupt or untrustworthy businessmen getting their hands on these fine institutions. The 'test' amounted to filling in a form. Article 10.4 asked applicants to declare many things, like whether they had been made bankrupt or had been admitted to hospital under the Mental Health Act (surely the fact that you have bought a football club would call that into question!).

One declaration that cause me to pause asked whether, 'he has been disqualified as a director pursuant to the Company Directors' Disqualification Act 1986 within the previous five years?'

I had been disqualified nine years ago. The disqualification had expired two years ago. I consulted with my lawyers. They were quite clear. There was no need to declare my disqualification. If it had asked whether I had served a ban within the last five years that would be different, but that wasn't what they were asking. Did I need to disclose it? The advice was no. I ticked the appropriate box, completed the form, had it sent to the SFA and forgot about it.

I had more pressing matters to deal with. An investigation carried out into my new board members had unearthed some damaging evidence.

Swift action was needed.

# EIGHT

POWER IS EVERYTHING. And now I had it, there were clearly people unhappy about it.

On the day after the takeover it was all smiles and warm handshakes – but I wanted to find out what was happening when my back was turned. Getting IT people to look at relevant emails on the internal server, sent before and after the acquisition, told me exactly that. That's when you see how two-faced people are.

On the one hand it's, 'Welcome, I really want to work with you'. On email it's something entirely different.

Reading the correspondence of some of the board members revealed they had reported me to police agencies on or around the day of the takeover, saying the money used to buy the club was from the proceeds of crime. A report was sent questioning my ownership of bus companies because they dealt in cash, and claiming I was friendly with criminal figures in Glasgow. They named one person I was friendly with who was apparently part of some organised crime network. To my knowledge he certainly wasn't. It was underhand in the extreme.

I'd had my suspicions about various people on the board throughout the negotiations, which was why I thought it prudent to have them checked out. We were able to access emails sent from their Rangers accounts. Now it was my company I had the right to check out who I was working with.

Of them all, Martin Bain was most careful. He rarely used his Rangers email. He preferred to use a private Hotmail account for certain correspondence. But, before the takeover, many of his all-rounder emails were copied to the rest of the board, excluding those he referred to as 'the pricks'.

He used his secretary to circulate emails to some of the others and that was how we could see what he thought of some of his colleagues under the David Murray regime. She asked if a particular message was to be sent to the whole board. Bain replied: 'Not to the pricks.'

We established this referred to Donald Muir and Mike McGill, the only ones who had enthusiastically encouraged the takeover.

There had been the matter of the independent board committee and the statement on the club's website questioning my suitability. Maybe I had reason to take action sooner, but I hadn't wanted to do anything before the end of the season. Such a distraction could have affected the team. But once the season was over I decided to take swift action.

I called a special board meeting. Gary Withey and I were the only ones in the boardroom. On a conference call were chairman Alastair Johnson, chief executive Martin Bain, finance director Donald McIntyre and director Paul Murray. In addition to the emails, we had evidence that Bain, McIntyre and Johnston had, in seeming contravention of the Companies Act, extended Bain's contract without shareholder approval and upped his salary 35 per cent to £633,000, including a bonus of £165,000. McIntyre and Bain were the only executive directors on salaries, so we took the decision to suspend them on the grounds of the financial irregularities.

The rest were non-executive directors. Johnston was due to be stepping down as chairman in the next two weeks. We asked him to resign immediately. He refused. We asked Paul Murray, the director who had launched a rival takeover bid, to resign. He refused. We terminated them both, which according to my lawyer we were allowed to do. They weren't at all happy. Martin Bain, who was in Idaho with Walter Smith, Ally McCoist and other backroom staff at a Rangers charity function, didn't say much.

The conference call was kept purposely brief and we said as little as possible – just that they were suspended from their employment pending further investigation. That was the legal advice we were given. Employment law can be quite complicated and the employer on the whole has a disadvantage against the employee so you've got to move fairly carefully, particularly when you have highly paid executives with long-term contracts.

John McClelland, who had been chairman from 2002 to 2004, and John Greig, the player voted 'the greatest ever Ranger' by supporters, were on the conference call. After the meeting I called them both and asked if they would stay on. Despite the fact they'd added their names to the IBC statement, I believed they weren't completely aligned to the others. They agreed to stay on.

Maybe there could have been a case made for reaching out to the people who didn't want me there, trying to keep them onside and trying to make it work. However, it was a matter of trust. It was important to establish control, but with a company like that maybe the best strategy would have been to get them all onside and make sure there wasn't this backbiting behind the scenes. I probably could have got Bain onside because he was on a lucrative salary, plus bonuses. Given I was the paymaster he probably would have done as he was told, but I just didn't trust the guy. McIntyre, too, could probably have been brought on side, but I didn't trust him and I've always had the opinion that I don't want to work with people I don't like or trust – and they all fell into at least one of those categories.

It was clear to me that Johnston, King, Bain and Paul Murray wanted David Murray out and for themselves to own the club. Paul Murray didn't seem to offer much and hung on the coat tails of people like King and Johnston. I don't think McIntyre wanted me there, but I didn't feel he was entirely affiliated with the others. McClelland, too, I suspected, would fly with the wind. Seeing how the key players had acted and how they viewed my takeover, I felt I had to take decisive action. One newspaper called it 'The Whyte of the Long Knives'.

However, I underestimated the bad feeling these people had. They had their own agenda. Bain and McIntyre both ended up suing the club and were eventually awarded payouts.

Dave King wasn't involved on the conference call. I met him for lunch at the Dorchester Hotel in London, not long after the takeover. I found him a bit of a sinister character. He played his cards close to his chest and didn't give much away about himself. He also never put his hand in his pocket. Every time we met for lunch I always paid. He didn't seem to like spending money.

He tried to convince me he could be helpful. He said he had provided short-term loans in the past to David Murray to keep things going when he had run out of money. He created the impression he would do that again but I knew that all his assets were frozen by the serious fraud office in the UK and it was unlikely he could put money into Rangers; and given he didn't want to pay for lunch, it didn't suggest he was going to be this generous benefactor.

He made it quite clear that his main interest in Rangers was to get his £20 million investment back. From a business point of view that was understandable.

David Murray might have agreed the flights but there was no formal arrangement. King reckoned he had got nothing for his £20 million other than his mother and his sister came to the games and went to the Blue Room every week. He thought he had bought two very expensive season tickets.

He was keen to make out that he could offer something but, as his money was still frozen in South Africa, part of me wondered if he was just gathering information to find out what was going on and to make sure I kept him on the board.

Shaking up the board allowed me to bring my own people in. Phil Betts was made a director, Gary Withey was the club's new company secretary. Andrew Ellis was also brought on as a director of the Rangers FC Group, upholding my end of the bargain from those early dealings, but he wasn't brought on to the Rangers board.

I also appointed Ali Russell as chief operating officer to focus on the commercial side of the business. Ali had sporting experience with the Scottish Rugby Union and at Hearts and Queens Park Rangers. Andrew Ellis, who knew Ali when he was at QPR, introduced us. I think Ali was hoping for a slightly calmer experience to the one he'd had working under Vladimir Romanov at Tynecastle. He had some bizarre stories of his time there. Rumours of Romanov's meddling in team selection were rife. They had resurfaced ahead of my first game in charge of the club. Apparently during one match Romanov actually wanted to come on in the last minute and play for the team. It sounded crazy.

When I had my first proper meetings with Ally McCoist as manager there was no danger of me asking to do that. Our meetings were constructive and friendly. I felt I got on well with Ally. I was mindful of the advice Murray had given about fostering a good working relationship with the manager. Ally set out his priorities – those on the current team he wanted to get signed up on longer contracts and what targets he had identified.

Walter Smith had been right about the number of players approaching the end of their contracts, so it was important to make sure we got those issues sorted quickly.

During the close season I moved to recruit Gordon Smith as director of football. My dad had long been friends with Colin Jackson, who played for Rangers for nearly 20 years during a rich period of success. Colin knew Gordon from their playing days together and introduced him to my dad, who mentioned him to me. As well as enjoying a distinguished career with Rangers and Brighton and Hove Albion, Gordon had worked as a football agent, TV pundit and latterly had been chief executive of the SFA. With his experience I thought he could lend support to McCoist on the player front, help develop the youth players and he could be my eyes and ears on the training ground.

Given the volume of leaks there had been from Ibrox, I was surprised news that I was meeting Gordon didn't come out, particularly when during one of our chats at the Hilton hotel the fire alarm went off and we had to stand outside. Not that it mattered in this case. As soon as I told Ally what was happening he was not at all happy with it. He wanted complete control. I'm sure that was what he had been used to during his career, dealing with one man, but modern clubs employed directors to help managers out. He never saw it that way though.

Another issue I had to address was a letter to shareholders, which I hoped might alleviate any fears some might have had about whether we were going to follow up on our promises. The letter was also an exchange for the waiving of the requirement buyers sometimes have to make a mandatory offer to all shareholders.

I informed them Wavetower Limited had been renamed the Rangers FC Group Limited. In the letter to shareholders, which was also posted on the club website, the Rangers group confirmed the commitment to waive the club's debt acquired as part of the takeover. The debt owed to Lloyds Banking Group, around £20 million, was now owed to Rangers FC Group. The Ticketus funds repaid Lloyds; Rangers FC Group guaranteed the Ticketus advance and undertook to waive that following a successful resolution of the tax case. The only way the debt wouldn't be waived was if the club lost the 'big tax case' with HMRC and lost any subsequent appeals.

We confirmed the undertaking to provide £5 million for investment in the playing squad and stated an intention to invest £20 million in the team by 2016. We confirmed the provision of a further £5 million of additional working capital to the club and the agreement to provide £1.7 million to fund capital expenditure to bring the catering facilities and the public address system at the stadium up to standard. I didn't put this in the letter, but when I looked ahead to the future I saw great potential for Ibrox. Although the main stand was a listed building there was scope to develop the surrounding area, which could certainly do with some regeneration. There were hotel, leisure and even residential options that could be explored. We were also keen to look at promoting Ibrox as a concert venue once more.

To shareholders, I confirmed the agreement to cover the £2.8 million liability owed from the discounted option scheme. We gave an undertaking to remain at Ibrox and continue with the training ground.

'As a keen Rangers supporter I look forward to helping the club secure its future as a leading force in Scottish and European football,' I said.

The letter was naturally picked up by the press and in a few quarters the reference to losing the 'big tax case' was perceived as me being open about the threat of insolvency.

For the most part, however, I hoped the letter would satisfy fans and shareholders that we were serious about our intentions and we could get on with the business of running the club.

The HMRC tribunal, which I hoped would take place very soon, was put back until November. I'd parked any thoughts of putting the club through a quick administration because of the impending tribunal. At least we had some months to focus on club business and my sense was that even if the tribunal went ahead we might be entangled in appeals and counter appeals for years to come. While part of me thought that might not be a bad thing, I didn't fully appreciate the damage the uncertainty would cause.

Before the takeover I hadn't given much consideration to the wider implications of being Rangers owner. I hadn't been in the job long when an invitation came to visit Bute House in Edinburgh to meet First Minister Alex Salmond. Ali Russell joined me for what was an informal chat. Salmond was friendly and welcoming. He is a self-confessed Hearts fan and has an interest in football. Plus he was trying to advance his new bill to clamp down on sectarian and offensive behaviour. The season just gone had been plagued by a number of unsavoury incidents – a fan had attacked Neil Lennon and bullets were sent in the post to the Celtic manager and two players. Parcel bombs intended for Lennon and his QC Paul McBride, who had also defended Celtic, had been intercepted. There had been incidents at an Old Firm match dubbed the 'game of shame'. I could understand where Salmond was coming from. I told him I was fully behind what he was trying to do, and that I realised Rangers had a responsibility to play our part. But I added that I did not want to see Rangers fans being singled out in any new legislation. The authorities were going to have to be very careful how they enforced this and it had to be across the board. Personally, I didn't think changing the law would change attitudes in the west of Scotland, but I reiterated my desire to continue the efforts that had been made at Rangers to stamp out unacceptable behaviour. It was a constructive meeting and interesting to see inside Bute House and how the Scottish Government operated.

I got another inside glimpse a couple of weeks later.

An article appeared in the one of the papers about football behaviour. Jack Irvine, who was now doing PR for me because there was no conflict with Rangers, said something critical of Alex Salmond and the government.

He was quoted saying: 'What we won't be is knocked around by knee-jerk politicians and by others across the city. We're drawing a line in the sand. Sectarianism is a problem, but it is not the sole problem of Rangers.'

Irvine reiterated what I said about Rangers supporting the First Minister's bid to rid Scottish society of bigotry and backing his decision not to rush through new legislation.

But Irvine added: 'There are elements in Glasgow and abroad desperate to lay the blame for Scotland's ills at the doors of Ibrox. I would have thought these politically-motivated critics might use their energies to analyse the chief problems in our society such as poor education, unemployment, drugs and youth crime. Respectable Rangers supporters – and that is the vast majority – condemn bigotry and sectarianism, but we will not be the whipping boys for society's failings. For too long, Rangers have taken it in the neck. Now it's a new owner, new management, new rules.'

Irvine's rant went on: 'I have a message for those who would denigrate Rangers – if you stop telling lies about us, we'll stop telling the truth about you.'

He was probably voicing what a lot of Rangers fans were thinking, but I was quite surprised to get a call from Alex Salmond at 9.30 a.m. one morning saying: 'What's this all about? What are you doing letting Jack Irvine talk about me in the press. Don't trust Jack Irvine. I've known him for years.'

The article hadn't even quoted me. There were certain similarities with David Murray in the way the First Minister monitored and dealt with coverage not to his liking. Obviously he was keen to have Rangers and Celtic backing his offensive behaviour bill, but essentially everybody I spoke to thought it was a load of crap.

I held a meeting with some members of an all-party Rangers Group at Westminster, which included John Robertson, the Labour MP for Glasgow North West, as chairman; Peter Robinson, the Northern Irish First Minister; Lord Wallace of Tankerness, the Advocate General; and Eleanor Laing, a Tory backbencher. It was agreed then that we needed to be more assertive. Secretary of the all-party group, Central Ayrshire MP Brian Donohoe, said the club should be on the offensive, not the defensive. We just wanted fairness.

It was fascinating to see how people of differing political persuasions had a common cause in their love for Rangers. The political reach of the club amazed me. And as a door-opener being the owner of a significant football club couldn't be beat.

For example, one of my colleagues at Merchant House, who was involved with the Conservative Party and the Democratic Unionist Party in Northern Ireland, said to me: 'You're not going to believe this. I've got a great deal for you. I have been talking to senior people in the DUP and they want to offer you a peerage so you can sit in the House of Lords for them, if you donate £250,000 and hold some functions for them in Northern Ireland.'

Peter Robinson was in the all-party group and I'd met some other DUP people at Ibrox. A huge contingent of support came over from Northern Ireland every matchday. The offer was on the table and if I had pressed the button it would have happened, but it wasn't something that interested me. When I look at the influence the DUP now have at Westminster, I think it's funny when you know the type of deals they've tried to make in the past. You wonder what else they have been up to.

Throughout the conversations to do with the offensive behaviour bill, however, my loyalty was to our fans.

One piece of advice David Murray gave me was never get involved with the supporters' groups. He thought they were a bunch of pricks. It was one of the first things he said to me. I couldn't see the harm in keeping them onside, so that was what I did. I spoke to them and they were all very keen for many of the traditional songs to be brought back. The 'Billy Boys' in particular, even though it had been banned by UEFA, they were desperate to sing again. It didn't make sense to me. Singing those songs had got us banned from Europe.

I did try to take a stand. I signed a letter that was handed to every fan before a home match, reminding them that they couldn't sing certain songs and of the consequences for the club if they did.

Another angle we looked at was bringing back 'The Billy Boys' but with a change of words. Gordon Smith had written some different wording but it was never going to work. Instead of 'up to our knees in fenian blood', he substituted 'media lies'. I had a chat with Gordon and Gary Withey about it, but we never put it to the fans.

The supporters' groups did agree to unite in condemnation of the most offensive songs and to eradicate chants about 'fenians' and the Pope from Ibrox. It was a step in the right direction.

However, it was important to make the fans feel we were taking them with us. Along with getting players signed up, season ticket sales were my main priority. By the end of June we had over 35,000 sold, up on our projections pre-acquisition and more than the club had at the same time the year before. It looked like the majority of them were buying into what we were trying to achieve.

On the playing side, early attempts to sign new players proved difficult. Other clubs took the view that when a team like Rangers showed an interest they could hold us to ransom. We were being quoted figures way above what players were worth. We had money to buy new players, but the days of spending over the odds had gone. It was frustrating because the fans wanted to see evidence that we were strengthening, but it wasn't for lack of trying. The transfer window system means players naturally want to hold out until the last minute, while agents have an over-inflated sense of their client's worth.

Shortly before the season started we went to Blackpool for a pre-season friendly. I had dinner with Owen Oyston, the club's owner. It was one of the more bizarre nights I had in my time at Rangers. He was surrounded by teenage girls as he offered interesting views on how to run a football club. He very much believed it should be run as a normal business. He refused to pay agents' fees, which sounded great if you could get away with it. He had no respect for managers or players, however. At one point after the game, Ally McCoist tried to get into the room we were in. He wasn't allowed and was told under no circumstances was he getting in. It turned into quite a late night. I think it was 2am before we left the stadium.

Our preparations for the new season didn't go exactly to plan when we lost three friendlies without scoring during a tour of Germany. We were then handed a potentially tricky Champions League qualifier against Malmo of Sweden. The season proper would have kicked off by then. We were at home to Hearts on the opening day, but it was clear we had to start strongly to cash in on European football.

There was some clamour from certain quarters for me to

stump up my own money to fund transfers. It would have been foolhardy for me to put my own money in, however, because there were so many issues still to be sorted. I was always clear with my advisors that no new money was coming in until we knew what was happening with the tax case.

We might have cut it fine, but new faces finally arrived. Ally's first new signing was the Spanish defensive midfielder Juan Manuel Ortiz, from Almeria. We then secured the services of one of the brightest prospects in Scotland, Lee Wallace, from Hearts for £1.5 million. Alejandro Bedoya was initially signed from Swedish club Örebro SK on a pre-contract arrangement to join in January, but we agreed a deal so he could come early.

While we were making plans to bring one of the new foreign players to Scotland, Sandy Jardine, the late, great Rangers' legend who worked for the club in a PR capacity, said: 'In the old days we used to send the chairman's jet to pick up players.'

I said: 'It's definitely changed days now. I don't have a jet and we won't be wasting money like that. They can come on Easyjet.'

In the build-up to the new season I gave some press interviews and recalled that glorious day in May when I was cheered into Ibrox. I added, however, that if things went wrong then I could be getting the opposite reaction one day. How prophetic those words proved to be.

The club worked hard over the close season to get Ibrox up to standard. There was still work to be done, but I hoped the fans who flocked there on the opening day would see some signs of improvement. The new state-of-the art sound system had been installed. We invested heavily in the Family Section of the Broomloan Road Stand and laid on pre-match entertainment for young fans.

Although we hadn't been in the door that long and had the essential repairs to tackle first, we quickly looked at a number of ways to build the Rangers brand and maximise our earning potential.

Since arriving at Ibrox, I'd discovered the club was shackled to a number of baffling deals. It was clear that under the previous regime anything that could have been sold off was sold off.

The club's retail arm and its internet presence were two examples of contracts that should never have been entered into. They had obviously got some money for them at the time but I was now saddled with these contracts.

Other contracts were costing the club needless amounts of money. A marketing company owned by Murray and Bain was receiving regular payments for handling season tickets. I wanted to cancel that.

Around £600,000 was being paid to the Murray group for administering the tax deal that they were still trying to collect money on after the takeover. There were numerous things that Murray hadn't told us.

I now understood why Murray had been reluctant to provide any warranties. There was no option open for us to go back to him now and claim the deal had been miss-sold.

I'd set aside my usual insistence on warranties when the deal had grown more attractive.

We'd got the company for £1 and with administration a distinct possibility I'd felt comfortable that even in a worst case scenario everything was protected. That was the thinking at the time, but already it was proving to be somewhat misguided.

I put those reservations to one side, though, and looked at how we could improve things short-term.

Once we managed to get the retail side of the business back under the club's control we could potentially make £5 million profit a year.

We looked at setting up a membership club for our global fanbase that would not only allow us to reach out and canvas people worldwide, but would also allow us to collect and utilise the data of hundreds of thousands of supporters for commercial potential.

In a similar vein, we considered expanding Rangers TV.

The previous regime had started to look at ways of redeveloping the area around Ibrox. We wanted to take these plans and progress them to see if it was feasible to have a hotel and retail village next to the stadium.

These were all ideas for the future. We hoped we would have enough time to start developing them.

Our priority, however, was making sure we were ready for the new season.

The day in July when we welcomed Hearts and got our first campaign under way was as beautiful and sunny as my first as owner. I had the honour of unfurling the league flag in front of packed stands, accompanied by 93-year-old Robert Andrew, a lifelong Rangers fan and season ticket holder for a remarkable 50 years. For a moment, as the fireworks went off behind me, I feared the flag wasn't going to budge. The press would have a field day if I messed this up. After a stiff tug, however, it came loose and fluttered in the breeze.

There might not have been a cloud in the sky – but storm clouds were gathering just over the horizon.

# NINE

WHEN I LOOK back on my time at Rangers, there are several moments that stand out as key to what lay ahead.

Being knocked out of the Champions League at the first hurdle was one of them, but it was the manner in which it happened that rankled with me. After losing the home leg against Malmo 1-0, we faced an uphill struggle in Sweden – and the UEFA ban meant the team was without the backing of any travelling Rangers supporters. Our task was made even greater when Steven Whittaker was sent off early on for stupidly throwing the ball at a Malmo player during a stoppage in play. What was he thinking?

Even after such a disastrous start, we gave ourselves a brilliant chance of qualifying when Jelavić scored to level the tie on aggregate before half time.

In the second half Madjid Bougherra was sent off for appearing to elbow one of their players on the back of the head. Malmo also had a player sent off. When players behave like that you often wonder if there's something else going on. Was it done on purpose? It's inexplicable. We tried to hold on, but lost an equaliser with just 10 minutes to go, meaning we were out of the Champions League.

Bougherra had already made it clear that he wanted away. As far back as March he had said he wanted to leave at the end of the season. He had been offered big money to play in Qatar. He was a good player and we wanted to keep him, but he basically downed tools until he got his move. We would end up getting £1.7 million for him, which was less than we thought he was worth, but he manipulated the situation until he could get away. That game in Malmo was his last for the club.

For Whittaker's misdemeanour, UEFA fined us €6000. I wanted to take the club fine off his wages, which we did, but then I had Ally McCoist telling me I couldn't fine a player €6000. He was on several thousand pounds a week. I did it on a point of principle. Eventually he was reimbursed the €6000. That's the mentality among the players. They don't want to pay for a thing.

Failing to reach the Champions League group stages cost the club between £15-20 million.

It was probably the moment when the inexperience of our young manager was most exposed. Had Walter Smith still been in charge and been able to guide us into the Champions League, I firmly believe I would still be the owner of Rangers today. Had our fans been there it might have made the difference. All consequences of events under the previous regime.

I might have been better persuading Walter to stay on, but he was costing £1.7 million a year, and McCoist was on £700,000 so we were saving a million per season. But with Champions League football worth up to £20 million, it would have been money well spent.

Champions League football would have bought us time to sort things out, rather than put us under pressure to get money in more quickly. The outcome would have been very different, both for Rangers and me. It wouldn't have ended in liquidation, I am certain of that.

Even Europa League football would have brought in £5-6 million, which would have kept us going for a few months longer, but even that was beyond us.

A 2-1 defeat by NK Maribor in Slovenia had given us a chance in the return leg at Ibrox, but we limped to a 1-1 draw and we were out of the secondary European competition, too. Celtic and Hearts also went out of Europe that same night, which highlighted how far Scottish teams had slumped in the years since Walter had guided Rangers to the UEFA Cup final. All I was really concerned about, however, was how it affected us.

Ally McCoist was untested as a manager, but I had no choice but to keep him as it would have cost the club £1 million to break his contract. My hands had been tied by the old board.

Frankly, the way the club had been run in the lead up to the takeover was incredible. To have had no provision for who would succeed David Weir, the captain, at the heart of the defence, was careless in the extreme. He was an excellent player, but it was obvious he wasn't going to last much longer as a first team regular.

It was even suggested to me by some that McCoist wasn't completely onside and was trying to sabotage things on purpose. I didn't believe it, but some people close to the team had a different point of view.

As a new football club owner there were some things I didn't profess to be an expert on. But to have a player flown to Eastern Europe to play a European qualifying match before the manager has even seen him play or train seemed bizarre. Yet that is what we did.

McCoist wanted Carlos Bocanegra, the USA captain. He signed him, flew him over and had him playing for the first team on the day he signed him, in a European qualifying match.

A lot of that might have been down to Ally McCoist's inexperience as a manager, but he had been assistant manager for Scotland and had been Walter's assistant for years. He should have known what he was doing.

Ally, did go out of his way to build a relationship between us, and we got on fine, but like anyone in that position, he played to the crowd as well.

Ally was never going to be convinced that a director of football was something he could benefit from. It was clear to me he needed help and we tried to help him, but what can you do when he ignores the man employed to do that?

It was indicative of the culture of a club that was set in its ways. Everyone you spoke to was stuck in the same mindset. We are Rangers. This is the way it has always been done. That attitude hung over every aspect of the club. It was ridiculous.

An example of this was on matchdays at Ibrox. Rangers had a room for the exclusive use of the directors before each game. I was shown it on my first day in charge. Instead of the directors mingling with ordinary fans, they went to their own special room with the directors of the visiting club. I thought it a bit odd. Clearly the Rangers directors had thought they were too good to mingle with ordinary people and thought they should be in an exclusive, more refined place. They thought quite a lot of themselves. As I was just in the door I didn't mention anything.

When the new season got underway, I realised Rangers were the only club that did this. We had another hospitality area, the Blue Room, with ornate, wood-panelled walls adorned with artwork of former players and a thick blue carpet. I thought that looked much more sociable, but convention dictated the directors kept to themselves.

At the start of the new season I kept up the tradition and went into the directors' room, but we permitted some other guests, some of whom were women. John Greig raised his eyebrows and said: 'Women aren't allowed in this director's room.'

That was Rangers through and through. It was a club that was set in its ways. Traditions like that hadn't changed in 80 years.

I said: 'It's my club and I can do what I want. I can invite the guests that I want.'

Greig might have been a former player, but I didn't consider him very sophisticated. After two or three games I couldn't stand it anymore. The directors' room was boring and lacked atmosphere, so I changed it. I moved everyone out of there. The Blue Room is at the top of the main marble staircase and that's where the most special guests are invited. Directors were allowed to invite about six guests, but I started to take the view that we should be inviting paying customers – people who were buying hospitality. Before then, it was always freeloaders who were in the Blue Room – former managers and players. I told the directors who were still there to get out and talk to the paying customers, the people who were in the hospitality suites. Get out there, say hello and talk to them. Nobody had ever done that before.

When I opened it up the new guests, the paying customers, were really pleased. We were spending a lot of money on match days, giving everybody free food and drinks, so why not reward those who are forking out for the club? It seemed simple, but normal business logic went out of the window at that club.

Rangers might not have attracted the same celebrity clientele as its neighbours. Celtic can boast Billy Connolly, Rod Stewart, Kevin Bridges, Jim Kerr and Frankie Boyle among their famous fans. However, that didn't stop us trying to attract some celebrities to Ibrox. Sean Connery was said to be a fan. He was a friend of David Murray. Sadly we weren't able to get him to a game.

We extended an invitation to Brad Pitt when he was in Glasgow filming *World War Z* in the city. Apparently the word back was that it would cost us £25,000 for him to come. I wasn't sure if that meant we'd get his then wife Angelina Jolie as well. If that had been guaranteed perhaps it would have been worth spending the money! I remember we were at home for a midweek game and although we weren't prepared to pay the appearance fee we still hoped he might make an appearance. What a coup that would have been.

Members of the DUP wanted tickets but didn't want to sit in the directors' box. They preferred to come incognito.

Jim Davidson came along to a match while he was appearing in panto in the city. He was very entertaining and knew a lot about the club. He seemed a genuine fan.

We often welcomed former players back to the club. Paul Gascoigne came to the Blue Room before a match, still as much of a character as I remembered from the times I took hospitality.

It was always good to see Ray Wilkins, who was as nice a man as everyone said. It's very sad to think he is no longer with us – his death was a huge loss to football.

There was an unwritten rule that directors can go and sit in on games at any other clubs and so we extended that same invitation to other clubs. I wasn't a big enough football fan to really take up the offer, but I did go to Stamford Bridge to see Chelsea in a Champions League game.

Largely, however, although we tried to create a different vibe around the club, it appeared that many of the stalwarts were more interested in traditions than progress at times. It was like walking into another world. Walking around the Blue Room, I've never had so many people try to give me a funny handshake – the tickle in the middle of your hand. Obviously I was aware of the club's Masonic links, but before I went in there as owner, I'd never really seen any evidence of it. Now I was in that position, people must have assumed I was one of them. I wasn't interested in any of that, but people must have thought I was part of it. Maybe I should have been. Almost everybody seemed to be part of a secret society, except me. It might have explained what was to come.

I remember meeting a sheriff in the Blue Room. There had been some reports at the time about the club facing legal action. He said: 'Call me if you ever need anything from the sheriff court. I'll do anything for Rangers.'

That surprised me. Maybe I should have made more use of offers like that. There was no doubt Rangers were considered the establishment club. A lot of the referees are obviously Rangers fans. We used to talk to them before the game and there was definitely a bias in some ways. We'd have a laugh and joke with them, saying things like, 'I hope you'll do us some favours today, make sure we don't lose here.'

I know some fans of other clubs think everything goes Rangers' way, but I find it hard to believe that they freeze the ball so Rangers get a home draw. It certainly didn't happen in my time there.

The influence over the press was something that surprised me, too. At the *Daily Record*, Bruce Waddell went out of his way to be friends. He called me and invited me to an awards night, Great Scots, in September, a black-tie function. I was sitting at his table. He seemed like a good guy. David Murray, being rather indiscreet, had told me Bruce would never have let him down, and he told me why. They had history together.

In the early days, if I wanted a story stopped I could get on the phone and stop it no problem. Almost no questions asked.

Jim Traynor used to send me his articles through before he'd print them, and I'd correct them for him. In the pre-internet days, Murray must have had complete control. Some journalists were happy to have a good relationship with Rangers if that meant getting stories, even if as a result it became difficult to criticise the club.

Traynor had got in touch through James Mortimer about a month after I went into Ibrox. We went for lunch at the Rogano restaurant and from that day he hounded me for a job. I know he denies this, but he begged me for a long time. He was desperate. I was never that impressed with him. I would soon discover he could fly with the wind.

I had dinners with all the editors and learned very quickly that if there was a negative story I could call some of them up and have a pretty good chance of getting it stopped. With the *Daily Record* I had a 100 per cent chance, and it was the same with *The Sun*. I used to call the editor of *The Herald*. I had a 50-50 chance of getting things stopped there. If it didn't get stopped, you threatened them with withdrawal of access, that they wouldn't get stories.

This is okay, I thought. This is control.

What was harder to control was the drip feed of leaks, both from inside the club and externally, to anonymous blogs online, which were then picked up by the media. It seemed any litigation we were involved in was appearing online. There was legal action from Martin Bain and an old lawyers bill dating back to the old regime. On top of that we had HMRC ramping up the pressure over the business of the 'small tax case'.

Leaked stolen papers relating to the Bain case suggested publicly for the first time that we could be facing a bill of close to £40 million in regards to the 'big tax case'.

The media attention wasn't something that sat easily with me. I'm a private, low-key person. But I only had myself to blame. Buying a football club had put me in the spotlight.

It was like there was a constant whispering campaign was undermining our ability to do business. I held a press conference to try to address some of the speculation.

When asked about whether the legal issues meant administration was a possibility, I said I wasn't going to speculate on what might or might not happen. But I added: 'That might be what's necessary. Sometimes you need to take a step back before you can move forward.'

There was still so much to be decided and a favourable outcome on both tax cases was still a possibility. The Bain papers had raised the spectre that Rangers could somehow be liquidated. I tried to alleviate fans' fears by saying: 'Rangers will come out of it stronger, whatever happens. Even in the worst-case scenario, Rangers will still be here.'

We had also come in for flak over our transfer window activity. Compared to the excess of the past it probably did look like we hadn't done much business. The truth was that before the transfer window shut we signed seven players and extended the contracts of seven others, spending £5 million on new recruits and new deals. We'd also rejected serious offers for players like Steven Davis and Nikica Jelavić, for whom we received a bid of £9 million on deadline day. Had it come in sooner we might have considered it, if we'd had time to get in a replacement, but it came in so late it would have left us short up front. We felt that refusing to sell two of our best players was a statement of our intent to fans that we weren't desperate.

That said, I thought it significant that we had been knocked out of the Champions League by Malmo, whose annual wage bill was just €5 million, significantly less than ours. We were then knocked out of the Europa League by Maribor, who had a wage bill of €1.5 million. One of our players probably got paid more than that. To me that said there was something badly wrong with the way things had been done. Instead of splashing out on expensive foreign players, we should have been focusing on our youth system to bring players through. There had been signs of encouragement with Gregg Wylde and Jamie Ness breaking into the first team, but we needed more of them to make the step up.

Crashing out of Europe so early meant we had to get on top of our cost base. We had to rid the club of the attitude that we could just throw money at things, that spending £5 million or £10 million on transfers every season was the done thing. Those days were gone. We'd spent £5 million, but had lost around £20 million through lack of Champions League football. Where was the sense in that? Surely it was better to develop young players.

There had been talk of league restructuring once again in Scotland – like that was going to solve all ills. The reality was that we had to cut our cloth accordingly.

The transfer window had been an eye opener. It was actually more difficult to spend money than I thought it would be. Of course there were things I could have handled better and I felt I'd be better prepared when the market reopened in January, but my priority had to be to get the best deal for the club. We weren't going to pay over the odds for anybody.

All the off-field speculation detracted massively from what was happening on the pitch. Despite our stuttering start in the league and European competition, we had put together a run of good results, winning five league games without conceding a goal. We were top of the table, but if we were to retain the title we couldn't afford many slip-ups. The first true test of our credentials would come with the visit of Celtic to Ibrox. The fans might forgive us for not making it further in Europe. Lose to our arch rivals, however, and it could be a long way back.

# TEN

IN THE WEEK building up to an Old Firm clash, when both Rangers and Celtic are up at top of the table, you might expect to see headlines about a 'dirty war'. Despite there being much at stake for both teams, however, all the talk was not about the traditional rivalry in Glasgow – but about a battle being waged with one of our former directors.

Martin Bain's decision to go to court to claim £1.3 million in lost earnings – claiming the club were on the brink of insolvency before a decision on the tax case – was designed to embarrass and, in my view, damage Rangers. At a time when we should have been preparing for the biggest domestic fixture of the season so far, focus instead was off the field and I was forced once again to go public to reassure fans we weren't going bust. Bain was granted an order in the Court of Session to freeze £480,000 of the club's assets.

McIntyre and Bain both froze bank accounts. Strange as it may seem, this is normal in Scotland. If you're the claimant, no matter how spurious the claim, you can freeze bank accounts. The other side then has to go back to court to get it lifted. It can't be done in England, only in Scotland. It should have been fought more vigorously and strategically we should have counter-sued them both. We didn't. It was a case of having other things to deal with first, but with the benefit of hindsight I should have taken a more personal approach with both employees.

People might look at what was to follow and think the claims against us were right, but at that moment there was nothing to suggest Rangers were in danger of liquidation. In fact making such claims in court contributed to a wider campaign against the club that seriously affected our ability to do business, which had major implications in the weeks and months ahead.

No one could say at that stage what the outcome of the HMRC tax case would be. We continued to fight the case and were working on a variety of options to limit the liability should the worst happen, but to have such allegations out there was harmful to the club's reputation. Bain always claimed to have the best interests of the club at heart, but such conduct was astonishing.

What also wasn't helpful were the comments from Peter Lawwell, the chief executive of Celtic, ahead of the game, pouring scorn on our claims of transfer interest in Jelavić. Lawwell said Celtic had received a £29 million offer for their striker Gary Hooper, 'from an unknown agent, from an unknown club, from another universe.'

I thought if the roles were reversed I'd be more dignified. It added to the spice of the occasion, but the truth was that relations between the two clubs were harmonious. It had proved beneficial over the years for the Old Firm to work together. Commercially, it made sense. We were keen to continue that relationship. Neither club would probably admit to it publicly, but they need each other.

I remembered Donald Muir's words before I was due to meet the old Rangers board at Auchenhowie, about Celtic having a 'much better bunch of guys'.

My first real contact with the Parkhead directors came when we hosted them at Ibrox. Despite Peter Lawwell's earlier digs, we got on well. There was some good banter before the game. Celtic are a well-run club, with a good team of directors, from interesting backgrounds. I'd invited a guest up to the game and he arrived carrying a briefcase. This was a gift for the Celtic fans. As they passed they all asked if he was the taxman. I jokingly chastised Peter for his fans winding up my guest. He said he was subjected to far worse whenever he encountered the Rangers fans.

I got a taste of what it was like when I travelled over to Celtic Park later in the season. We parked by a nearby school and the police escorted us in. It was pretty intimidating, walking past several hundred jeering fans.

At Ibrox, the first Old Firm derby of the season ended in a 4-2 win for Rangers after both teams lost earlier leads. I couldn't relax until we'd got the fourth goal. Even though we'd got ourselves back in front at 3-2, I was convinced Celtic would nick an equaliser. It was a hugely significant result. Not only was it Ally McCoist's first Old Firm victory as manager, but it also opened up a four-point lead at the top of the league. It was particularly sweet as we'd had to endure the Celtic fans trying to turn the occasion into a party. They'd lapped up the negative coverage we'd suffered over the legal cases. In addition, Celtic had been extremely fortunate in Europe. Although they had been beaten soundly by FC Sion 3-1 over two legs, UEFA found the Swiss side guilty of fielding ineligible players and excluded them from the competition. Celtic took Sion's place in the group stage of the Europa League. Gleeful Celtic fans had brought along beach balls and the like to rub it in – they were still in Europe, while we'd crashed out. So to get one over on them was brilliant, and you could see what it meant to the Rangers fans. The place was jumping. This is why I got into this, I thought, as I watched the fans stream out, huge smiles on their faces.

The police reported that, aside from a few minor disturbances, the game passed off peacefully. After the events of the previous season, and given the level of scrutiny on the fixture in light of the Scottish Government's proposed bill, that was a welcome relief. My aim that football should and could be an entertaining way to spend an afternoon or evening without fear of violence or clouded in sectarianism didn't seem so fanciful.

A couple of days after the game Peter Lawwell called me to talk about how both clubs could get out of Scotland and into English football or another more lucrative league. It was an issue that had raised its head many times in the previous few years. The key point, however, was that in the short term the English leagues didn't want Rangers and Celtic. I was all for exploring every option. Anything that expanded commercial opportunities and improved Rangers' chances of competing with the biggest clubs south of the border and in Europe was worth looking at.

The idea that I came up with was starting at the very bottom of the English League set-up, possibly a side in the Conference, or National League as it's now called. You would rebrand them as Rangers, kit them out in blue, white and red and work your way up the leagues. At some point you would merge both clubs and have the 'English' team play in Glasgow. It was pie-in-the-sky stuff and fraught with issues, but the potential gains were huge and worth further investigation.

Banstead Athletic, a small club in Tadworth, Surrey, in the Combined Counties League, could have fitted the bill. Through a business associate called Aidan Earley, we looked at doing some cooperation, with Banstead as a feeder club that could be branded in the future. There were no detailed discussions with

Banstead, however, and certainly no money changed hands, as was later reported. We also had initial conversations with the agent Willie McKay who said he was acting for Doncaster Rovers. He said they would be interested in doing a deal. This sounded attractive as ideally we would have wanted to work with a club that was in the Football League. We did not speak to anyone from the club directly and there was no time to progress the plan.

In the English Premier League Rangers would have been worth £500 million. Right now it was worth close to nothing. Had I the chance to plan long-term, a route to England would have been uppermost in my mind, as it is in the mind of Dermot Desmond, Celtic's single biggest shareholder, and Peter Lawwell. Unfortunately the Premier League doesn't want Rangers or Celtic. Those clubs might not have had the final say, though. If the big television companies insisted on it as part of a lucrative new package, then the decision might be taken for them.

There was also talk of an Atlantic or Nordic league, but nothing came of it.

A more realistic hope was that the Europa League expanded to such an extent that European football was the main source of income and there were far more guaranteed matches. The bigger clubs were exploring that. I still think that is likely to happen.

Most Premier League teams tend to treat each other pretty well. When you travel to away games you get good hospitality, just as visiting directors were warmly welcomed at Ibrox. Everybody was very friendly – win, lose or draw. Generally we were winning, so you were commiserating with the losing team. Some of the directors I knew from business connections in the past, like Stewart Milne, the chairman of Aberdeen. It was interesting to bump into him again years after we'd done business together. The vice-chairman of Motherwell at the time, Derek Weir, used to go to the same school as me – I was in the same year as his brother – and we grew up on the same street.

It was quite amusing when the representatives of smaller clubs came to Ibrox. When we played Dunfermline, they brought guests with them and they wanted to see the trophy room and be shown around the ground. Some even wanted their photo taken with me. I suppose it reinforced the feeling for some that Rangers were something special and far bigger than the other clubs.

Probably the most colourful character in the league was Vladimir Romanov, but he had stopped going to the games by the time I took over. Ali Russell suggested I go to Lithuania to meet him, but I couldn't see what I'd get from it.

Mike McGill claimed to me that a couple seasons before I got involved Romanov offered to throw a game for cash in order to help Rangers win the league. I didn't know the ins and outs of the offer, but whatever the reason, the offer wasn't entertained. The story sounded very bizarre, if indeed it was true. How would it even be possible to pull off?

I almost wished it were so easy to manipulate results as just four days after the high of beating Celtic we came crashing back down to earth with a shock 3-2 defeat away to Falkirk in the League Cup. Once we'd gone out of Europe, a run in each of the cups was even more crucial to generate some revenue over the course of the season. Seeing our challenge for the first silverware of the year crumble so early was hard to take. Football certainly was a rollercoaster of emotions.

I was still based in London and going to the office at St Paul's every day, but Rangers were taking up a lot more of my time than I expected. I was getting sucked into so many different things, there were so many PR crises I felt I should get involved with. I regret ever speaking to the media. I should have kept out of it and remained a bit of a mystery, but I was dragged into it and it was now taking up too much of my time

The way things were going, it often seemed that events on the pitch played second fiddle to those off it. Donald McIntyre, suspended since May, formally resigned from his post at the start of October and promptly sued for damages. Shortly afterwards John McClelland and John Greig resigned from their non-executive positions on the board. They claimed they had been isolated, but the reality was their positions didn't afford them the privilege of being involved in the corporate governance of the club.

A story circulated that I wanted rid of John Greig. It was simply nonsense. Although he must have been unhappy at some of the changes I made around Ibrox, I felt we always got on well together and when I spoke to him before his resignation he did not express any problems or mention anything untoward to me. His resignation therefore took me by absolute surprise. My view was that he was and always would be a great Rangers man. His statue outside the ground stood testament to the esteem in which he was held, so I was disappointed to see him go and hoped he would continue to come to the games. He was the greatest-ever Ranger and as such would always be welcome. I never suspected either of them was that wedded to the old board, so I queried the timing. I was beginning to conclude that nothing should surprise me in football. John McClelland never spoke to me either, before his decision. I didn't have an opportunity to address any of their reasoning head on.

It was one thing after another. I was living in London and Monaco and the intention had been to only come up to Scotland when necessary, but the raft of issues affecting the club and the never-ending speculation meant it was a constant battle to keep on top of the inaccurate reporting.

I was under scrutiny and felt pressured to speak to journalists. The club had its publicity machine, but I was now in a mindset that I could sort it, driven perhaps by the early success I'd had in controlling the story. I felt we always needed to make sure we got our side across. And between May and September, despite some setbacks, things had gone pretty well and I was encouraged and fairly confident that we could make the business work.

Around this time Ken Olverman, Rangers' financial controller came to me and said Dave King had asked when we were going to pay his expenses.

He had an arrangement where the club routinely paid for him to travel first class from South Africa to Scotland three or four times a year. I said we wouldn't pay them.

King sent me several emails asking why I wasn't paying them. He was very upset about it.

My thinking was that further changes might have to be made.

But as we entered October two hugely significant events holed my ambitions below the waterline.

The first was when David Grier informed me that he and his partners had sold MCR – the corporate restructuring firm that was a part of the takeover process and had handled the bank debt – to Duff and Phelps, a huge American financial services company with offices all over the globe. I didn't even know they were selling the firm. Initially, I didn't think much of it. He continued to advise me and our original agreements were still in place. However, although they were engaged and continued to be funded by Rangers they seemed to be doing little. I had no inkling of the ramifications the sale of MCR to Duff and Phelps would have both to my future and that of Rangers.

Maybe I would have attached greater significance to the move had I not been distracted by a forthcoming documentary BBC Scotland were planning.

A perfect storm was building, one that would soon engulf me entirely.

# ELEVEN

THE BBC WAS founded on many principles, one of which was fairness. When BBC Scotland decided to investigate my background for a documentary in October 2011, it didn't seem that principle was afforded to me. The reporter behind it was a respectable journalist whose previous investigations meant the programme carried considerable weight. In my opinion, however, it was a hatchet job.

It levelled three main charges against me – that I had been disqualified as a director, that potentially I could have faced criminal charges for continuing to perform as a director while disqualified, and they had unearthed a disgruntled former business associate who complained I hadn't done enough to save his firm.

It wasn't so much what they said, but the way they said it. It was made to sound far worse than it was. Of course I couldn't deny I had been disqualified. It was just unfortunate that it came to light in such a manner. The company they highlighted was going back 18 years. It was a security company that had been acquired and eventually became a minor subsidiary of the Custom Group. It ran into difficulties and stopped trading. A rescue package was put together, all the jobs were saved and put into a new entity. It was a sensible restructuring, which happens on a regular basis. Turnarounds are messy. You take a firm through the insolvency process and some people get hurt. It's not ideal, but insolvencies happen all the time. I didn't get the criticism.

I wasn't a director of the company, but it led to the disqualification. Suddenly I wished I'd fought it at the time, but I had no idea that decision was going to come back and bite me in such a public arena. Besides, it was ancient history. It had no relevance to what was happening at Rangers.

In terms of whether my actions could have resulted in criminal charges, that accusation came from one financial investigator. If it had been so serious, why hadn't I been investigated at the time?

I was aware that the BBC were making a documentary weeks before it aired, but I was not aware of the contents until a couple of days before transmission. It seemed like a muck-raking exercise and continued a general theme of negativity since I'd taken over. We'd already had cause to withdraw cooperation with the BBC in July over a report into the sectarian issue, where they'd segued comments about violence and the behaviour of fans with completely unrelated footage of Ally McCoist smirking, taken from *A Question of Sport*. They later apologised for that.

I tried to take the same tack now. I denied any wrongdoing, restated my commitment to the long-term security of the club and immediately stopped all cooperation with the BBC, threatening to sack any employee who broke that order.

I also banned *The Herald* at one point, but interestingly the journalists from the other papers, who hadn't been that bothered about the BBC's restrictions, suddenly got upset and claimed it wasn't the way to carry on. They probably had a point. It wasn't constructive to ban the media, but when you're in control and the media have annoyed you, it's the easiest thing to do.

I thought I could just bat it away. I wanted to control everything that was in the media. I'd had some success at getting articles I didn't like pulled or edited favourably so, bizarrely, I thought I could control the agenda.

I was wrong. The programme was hugely damaging. I felt like the boy with his finger in the dam. But for how long could I hold off the flood waters?

I'd announced the ban before the programme aired, which might have had the unfortunate consequence of drawing more attention to it. Certainly the other media had a field day. One small, but not insignificant, consolation was that the Rangers fans chanted 'Fuck the BBC' during a game. Around 100 fans later staged a protest outside BBC Scotland's Glasgow HQ. At least some of them were adopting a siege mentality – something they'd develop strongly in the years to come.

Another consolation in the wake of the documentary was hearing that the DUP's Peter Robinson had got in touch to ask if he could help in any way. He'd had his own public relations issues over the years and he got in touch via our mutual contact, saying that he knew what it was like and if I wanted him to come and be photographed next to me at Ibrox he would do that. He sounded like a decent guy.

I was conflicted over how to play it publicly. After employing a strategy of trying to be open, I should have gone in front of the media and explained fully the situation. I should have given my defence regarding the disqualification. But I didn't. I tried to shut it down, like I'd been able to in the past. That was the opportunity to be up front about the documentary charges and the financial crisis. With the tax case, I could have said things were going to be difficult. We were going to have to tighten the reins for a bit, but we would be here to take things forward.

I should have said that from day one. And then I should have got my head down and not said anything until I'd resolved the issues.

However, I had David Murray pretending we had done this brilliant deal that was going to bring a load of money into the club. That was how they wanted to spin it to the media, and I went along with that. Secondly, I wanted nothing that might discourage Rangers fans to buy season tickets as that was crucial to our cash flow.

What the fans didn't appreciate was that we'd been doing everything we could to try to maximise revenue, but we seemed to be stymied at every turn.

As soon as we'd done the deal to settle the outstanding debt with the bank, albeit to the new company instead, of the club, they didn't want to know. The Bank of Scotland, part of Lloyds Banking Group, withdrew all the overdraft facilities even though we had repaid the debt in full with the Ticketus advance. They didn't want Rangers to even have an account. They wanted Rangers gone. They wrote a letter basically telling us to piss off.

The only reason we didn't was because we couldn't find any other bank that would take our account. We spoke to Clydesdale, HSBC, two or three others. It wasn't as though we were asking for an overdraft – they didn't even want the account. It was incredible. The climate was so grim that banks didn't want to touch a football club, even if it was in credit. They were scared of the publicity if the bank were somehow blamed for something going wrong.

We were looking at other investments or business opportunities, but the BBC programme, coming in the midst of the tax case, added to the uncertainty surrounding the club. Having my business acumen questioned, unfairly in my opinion, in such circumstances stopped some negotiations we had about raising more money. In other cases it slowed things down when we didn't have the time to spare. For instance, we were looking at a sale-and-lease-back arrangement for the training ground that could have brought in £10 million, with an option to buy it back in the future.

Who would enter into a five-year deal when there was so much to be resolved?

During this period, we were actively trying to resolve the tax case and work out a contingency plan should the worst happen and we lose the case and be faced with a £49 million bill.

Conversations had taken place on how we could raise additional money. There was one offer for a stand-by facility to pay the 'big tax case' liability. It was an American hedge fund. There would have been a fee for setting up the facility, but that would have been extremely helpful. We were negotiating along those lines.

We tried to have a conversation with HMRC before the tribunal was heard. We went to them and said, 'Let's just assume the worst, that we lose the case. Let's have the collection discussion now. If we lose the case, what will the deal be? How long will we have to pay? Can we pay it over 10, 20 years? Whatever it is, let's have the conversation now. That would then give us clarity to speak to other investors and know how we would be moving forward.'

We could have gone out to the stock market and said, 'This is the worst-case scenario for the club – we owe HMRC £50 million and we've agreed to pay it off at £2.5 million-a-year, plus interest'. If we'd had to pay it back at £5 million-a-year it would have been a push, but at least we would have known what we were dealing with. We had some fantastic assets, a huge, loyal fan base, we had great potential for investors. It wasn't so outlandish to think we could have raised £20-30 million from a share issue. Maybe we'd have had to put prices up, sell some of our assets, or ask the fans to help out. We could have found a way, but at least we would have had certainty – that would have been our worst-case scenario.

If we could have done that Rangers would have survived, but HMRC refused to have that discussion. What we were trying to argue was they could still have set a precedent and discuss how we'd go about settling matters. It's difficult to fathom why they wouldn't want to have that discussion, because it wouldn't have prejudiced them in any way whatsoever. I think they were keen to be seen not to be giving Rangers preferential treatment. But this was not preferential treatment. This was someone saying, 'We owe you some money – let's talk about how we are going to pay it back'. How would that prejudice anybody?

It didn't make sense to me, but we weren't dealing with commercial people. They didn't seem to care as long as they got their money.

I hadn't expected this attitude at all. From the moment I took over, I was confident that we'd either win the case or be able to do a deal with HMRC. In my experience, when it came to dealing with HMRC, there was always a deal to be done. They always wanted to get paid and David Murray's thoughts were the same.

That all changed in November, when I went to a meeting with their top people in Edinburgh.

We talked about the tax case and other tax issues with the club and they said, 'If Rangers win this tax case, we will appeal, appeal, appeal, until we win.'

I realised then there was no chance of a deal. My assessment of the situation had been wrong.

My mind went back to the conversations I'd had with members of the previous board about HMRC. The view around Ibrox had strongly been that HMRC 'were all Tims out to get us'. That was a direct quote from somebody. I remembered David Murray's assertion that the man in charge,

Keith McCurrach, was from a big family of Celtic supporters. Now that I was dealing with them face to face, I sympathised with that mindset. Gary Withey actually asked McCurrach directly: 'Are you doing this because you're a Celtic fan?' He said: 'No, don't be silly. I hate football.'

It was a completely unprofessional thing to ask, but it gave an indication of the frustration we felt that there was no willingness to even meet us halfway. They just seemed to be so obstructive that there had to be something driving it.

Whatever the motivation, we had a real issue on our hands now.

The dam was bursting.

We had legal action from Martin Bain and Donald McIntyre, we had HMRC freezing the bank accounts for money that was due. The money we'd taken from season ticket sales in the summer – around £12 million to £15 million – was being used to pay the bills, but those funds were dwindling and due to run out in March.

We were desperate to put some pressure on HMRC, and I went through to Edinburgh to see Alex Salmond at Bute House for a second time. Quite interestingly, he said: 'HMRC are incompetent.'

I could agree with that.

He went on: 'I'm happy to call the head guy at HMRC and help you out with this.'

There was a caveat.

'I'll do this for you, providing you put out a statement on behalf of Rangers in support of the offensive behaviour bill.'

He did speak to the HMRC and tried to take the pressure off, but it failed. And I never put out a statement in support of his bill.

It was interesting how being in charge of a football club carried influence with politicians. They know you can speak to a large section of the public, so they want to be your friend.

I still used to speak to David Murray every week. He would call me and ask how things were going. He never wanted to speak on a mobile, always on a landline. We had a decent relationship at that point. During such conversations he came across as a guy who wanted to be helpful. The mood changed though when I broke it to him, around October or November, that I didn't think we could avoid administration.

He started to panic. I think at that stage he knew this was going to reflect badly on him.

'You need to do everything you can to avoid it,' he said.

It wasn't like I wasn't trying. Although we'd looked at it as a possibility at the time of acquisition and it had been referred to in the share purchase agreement, by the end of October I had been looking to do anything but put the club into administration. However, after the meeting with HMRC it went from a possibility to being highly likely.

We had a conversation quite early on with the SFA about doing a solvent restructure. We spoke to the Scottish Premier League lawyers, Harper Macleod, and said we were considering doing a restructuring and putting all the assets into a new company on a solvent basis, so it can continue if the tax case goes wrong. They seemed to think it was something that could work. This was back in October. We could have all the assets in a new company but there would have been no financial penalty, or even a points penalty.

We could have restructured into a new company and left the old company behind. All that was needed was a vote from the other member clubs for that to happen. And they were more than likely to agree to that now than they would be against the backdrop of all the fury and fan pressure that would come with an administration.

However, we didn't have the time to pursue it, because, as with everything to do with football, you can't just do things unilaterally like you can with other businesses. You've got to get the agreement of the officials in the league and the board members, made up of representatives from other clubs. It was far tougher than any other business and it is one of my regrets that I didn't pursue it more stringently at the time. If we had worked then on gaining a tacit agreement from the other clubs then we could have had a very different outcome.

By November 5 we were sitting at the top of the league, 12 points clear of Motherwell, who were in second, and 15 ahead of Celtic, the most likely challengers come the end of the season, in third.

I thought there was a chance we could be in and out of administration quickly. We'd probably incur a 10-point penalty, but we could exit administration and still be top of the league. The debt would be gone. I was relaxed about the prospect. It was probably beneficial for the club to go into administration. I would keep control. By entering administration we'd get rid of the tax debt; we'd get rid of all the bad deals that Murray had done over the years, such as the retail contract other contractors that were signed up for long periods of time. We'd get out of all of that. Any players we didn't want? We could terminate their contracts as well.

In my experience of other businesses I'd taken through that process, there was nothing to fear. It was a positive option. I thought I could ride the publicity. My hope was that any negativity would generally be aimed in David Murray's direction.

Another significant factor was the advice from MCR – now Duff and Phelps. Although they hadn't been able to do what they promised and negotiate an agreement with the bank, they were my preferred administrators in the event we went down that route.

They told me if we went into administration they wouldn't allow HMRC's claim. This was important because HMRC had a claim for £75 million. Not allowing their claim meant that HMRC wouldn't have had a vote to stop a company voluntary agreement (CVA) – which you need to emerge from administration – from going through. Their grounds for disallowing HMRC's vote was that the case hadn't been decided yet.

So I was looking at a situation where there was a good chance I could get a CVA through and we could have emerged from administration, with the team still top of the league, debt free and I would still be in charge.

What's not to like about that?

It looked a viable scenario.

I had a conversation with Ally McCoist in the manager's office. I told him: 'I'm seriously thinking about putting the club into administration. We're 12 points clear in the league now. We could have a 10-point deduction. If you still win the league you'll go down as the best manager in Rangers' history.'

'Go for it,' he said.

I should have taken his advice. I should have gone for it then. I probably bottled it. I was still concerned about taking the club through administration when it might not be necessary. We might still win the tax case, but the First Tier Tribunal had been postponed once again, this time to January. Our lawyers believed we still had a good chance of winning that case. However, the failure to act was my responsibility.

What became clear is that my advisers on the tax case seemed to be developing a relationship with HMRC.

# TWELVE

31 JANUARY 2012 – transfer deadline day and the culmination of a crazy month spent dealing with unrealistic fan expectation, hyped up by a media living on another planet.

Given the precarious position we were in, the sale of our top goalscorer Nikica Jelavić, regretful though it was, to Everton for around £6 million made sound business sense. Out of Europe and with cash dwindling, we had to try to rein in our spending, while maximising the potential of any saleable assets. The player wanted to leave and there was no point in trying to keep someone who no longer wanted to be at Ibrox. Several clubs were interested in him, and some Championship sides offered more than we eventually received, but he wanted to play in the Premier League and the offer from Everton represented a good return on our original investment.

However, in the eyes of pundits, former Ibrox legends that wanted to voice an opinion – of which there were many – it was probably the moment we lost the league title.

It was also the day the *Daily Record* revealed the Ticketus deal.

Taken in isolation, with an otherwise fair wind, it might have been possible to explain the rationale behind the arrangement.

Coming as it did amid a maelstrom of speculation, sniping from the sidelines and legal cases left, right and centre, it was the spark that lit the blue touch paper.

In December, Bruce Waddell had been removed from his position as editor at the *Daily Record*. At the time I didn't attach much significance to the change. I should have done. I never met the man who took over, but Jim Traynor did tell me the incoming editor didn't like me. I didn't know why that was the case, but it seemed he didn't like the new set up at Rangers.

Waddell had obviously valued the relationship he had with Murray and wanted that to continue that with me, but the new editor didn't seem to be interested in that kind of relationship. Although we tried to control the negativity through Traynor, we had less success than before. Given the *Record* had seemingly known the details of the Ticketus deal months earlier, it was slightly surprising it took them until the end of January to look at it again. Maybe I should have seen there was a potential problem looming, with a new regime in place, but there was so much else going on. When the story came to light, we weren't in a position to limit the impact. They splashed it over five pages, interestingly also harking back to their initial description of me as a 'billionaire' – something that was their own original mistake. This time they blamed Hay and McKerron for misadvising them. I don't know if that was the case. To me it was journalists not understanding the difference between personal wealth and money under management. Again, something small at the time now blown up looked very damaging.

I tried to defend our position, explaining that the Ticketus model had been in place under the old regime. I reminded fans that the biggest issue remained the tax case, the uncertainty from which was still hampering our ability to do business.

But the issue of my trustworthiness became the story.

Paul Murray and Alastair Johnston came out of the woodwork to suggest all their warnings had come to pass. Murray had already claimed days earlier that he was puzzled that administration was even being considered now, questioning what had happened since the summer to suddenly make cash flow an issue when the tax liability still wasn't known.

He must have conveniently forgot that Johnston had raised the issue of administration as recently as April. It also must have slipped his mind that he was on the board when the club got itself into this mess in the first place.

This was the same Paul Murray whose last ditch offer for the club had amounted to a five-line email sent from his Blackberry. His deal was built around a £25 million share issue underwritten by backers he would not name. If it had been remotely credible, David Murray or the bank wouldn't have dismissed it.

It all stemmed back to the fact that he and Johnston might not have liked me taking over, but they didn't want David Murray to remain in charge either. They had their chance to save the club when Murray announced he was looking to sell. Both had failed to find a saviour. What Paul Murray had to say should have been irrelevant. Sniping from the sidelines wasn't helpful or constructive, but it now became a national sport.

Nothing seemed to be going right.

By the end of the year, our lead at the top had evaporated and a narrow defeat at Celtic Park had seen our rivals leapfrog us at the top of the table.

The SFA had announced it was investigating whether I passed a fit and proper test over the director disqualification.

Trading in shares was suspended because we had been unable to produce audited accounts due to the delays in the tax tribunal. We had been considering changing the club's status as a listed company anyway. With 85 per cent of the shares owned by a single company, there was hardly any trading in the remaining 15 per cent, and therefore little tangible benefit for the club to be a listed company. The reality was a public listing simply meant more bureaucracy. That didn't seem to matter. Even before the *Record*'s revelations it had got to the point where every new development was billed as a 'blow for Rangers' regardless of whether it had any material impact on the running of the club or not.

On the pitch, too, we suffered bad luck. We had already lost Steven Naismith to injury for the rest of the season when Kyle Lafferty was also crocked.

Gordon Smith did a good deal to bring in Sone Aluko, who made an immediate impact. He didn't cost any money and under normal trading circumstances the club would have been looking to make a decent return when the time came for him to move on.

Investment in the squad had continued to be a thorny issue and was the source of endless debate, most of it ill-informed. Due to the contractual state of the squad we had inherited we had conducted 14 different pieces of transfer business, a combination of new signings and improvements to existing contracts with key players – more than any other club in Scotland. We had brought in eight or nine players, increased the players' wage bill significantly and boasted a first-team squad of 30, which included 18 full internationalists.

Regardless of that, the narrative was that we had done nothing.

In the early part of the season, when the team had been doing well, I was reasonably happy to leave Ally and the coaches to the playing side while I concentrated on the business side of things.

When the performances started to dip I started to look at the playing set-up more closely.

The life of a football player looked a cosseted one. It appeared to me as though they didn't do much. I'd go into the training ground at 2.30pm and the place was dead. That got to me. I was paying these players a lot of money. They had the use of a state-of-the-art facility, run at considerable expense, and there wasn't a soul there.

As far as I could tell, they got in to training at 10.30am, had a run around the pitch, got their free breakfast, their free lunch and then they disappeared. What a life.

As a businessperson, I was used to employing people I expected to work hard. So why was there little evidence of them doing anything? Where were the double sessions, the extra time spent working on tactics, formations or set-pieces? To my untrained eye there didn't seem to be any additional work being put in. It was frustrating, signing off the payroll every month to these guys, when they weren't doing it on the pitch every week.

I'm sure there were exceptions, but in the main footballers struck me as mercenaries. They were there for the money, not because they loved the club.

We had players making £10,000 to £20,000-a-week and, for some, all that money brought problems.

I used to hear all sorts of things about the players. The club doctor told me a player had picked up a sexually transmitted disease and his performances had seemed to dip as a result.

At a time when we needed the players to be at the top of their game, the form of the team nose-dived. Possibly the events off the pitch had a bearing, but they were professionals. They should have been able to shut that out.

It didn't help, though, when you had media coverage that bordered on the hysterical, particularly throughout the transfer window.

In a statement to reassure fans I said we had to be realistic.

Rangers had operating costs of approximately £45 million a year and revenues of around £35 million – which didn't include revenues from possible Champions League and Europa League participation. Without European money there was a big financial hole to fill every year – regardless of who owned the club.

We had to move on from the mindset that we had to keep spending more and more money. That was what had got the club into financial trouble in the first place. We had to live within our means, continue to develop talent and spend wisely.

I told fans I had a £25 million personal stake in the club and would do all I could to make sure we stayed successful – that was all true; I had a personal guarantee to Ticketus for £25 million which was enforced

Despite the doom and gloom, the league title was still there to be won and a Scottish Cup run might have helped lift the mood. A fifth round defeat at home to Dundee United, however, not only left us with one chance of silverware, but also deprived us of any further income.

Amid this malaise I had to deal with changes to the board. Phil Betts wanted to resign as a director. He was under pressure from his family and was uncomfortable with the scrutiny and attention. I tried to talk him out of it. He was a valuable ally but he was adamant. He probably could see the way it was going to go and, quite sensibly, wanted to avoid the fall out. His decision did not affect our friendship and we remained good mates. In fact it was probably the best decision he has ever made.

I brought Andrew Ellis on to the board as a non-executive director. I think he thought he was going to be running the club, but the reality was he didn't offer me much.

We tried to get rid of Dave King around this time. Gary Withey had a meeting with him where he was told we wanted him to go. He managed to talk Gary round though, who in turn convinced me we might as well leave it. That was a mistake – because he was never going to be onside with us.

The club was so paralysed by events and speculation that I took further advice regarding entering administration. The legal advice was that we had to serve a notice of intention to put the club into administration and then we had two weeks where we could make plans and sort out whether it was actually going to go into administration. That action stalled any creditor payments for those two weeks. And the advice assured us that such a situation was unchallengeable. There was even scope to extend for a further two weeks. That would have given us a month to sort out some kind of solution. My preferred administrator was Duff and Phelps, who I believed were still working on my behalf. I had capped Duff and Phelps' administration fees at £500,000. In my experience administrators had been quite adept at taking any money that was available. I thought capping the fees was in the best interests of the club.

Additionally, I planned to make sure there was no money left for them to take. If they weren't able to take anything in fees, they would have to continue dealing with me.

The two-week window could have given us a chance to restructure the company. There was even a chance we might not have had to go into administration at all. We could have planned a notice of intent to go into administration and then sorted it out in that two- or four-week period. In the event that we did go down that route, my view was that we should enter administration in the morning and exit in the afternoon. I didn't envisage a long process. Duff and Phelps would have been forced to do that if we had this notice of intention. They would have had to work with me or with another buyer if one came forward, to make sure their limited fees were paid.

That was the plan.

On February 12 we filed the notice of intention to appoint administrators. The following day, HMRC lawyers went to court to try and appoint their own administrators. HMRC were worried that we would soon be issuing another payroll. By that stage, the club was not paying PAYE or National Insurance contributions. I could see why they were concerned, but given their refusal to enter any negotiations with us about the payment of tax bills, there wasn't much else we could do.

Our notice of intention should have given us full protection from creditors. This means that during this period creditors couldn't have demanded any money. Under these circumstances, any normal creditor would stop supplying the company with goods or services during this period. HMRC, however, are not like any other creditor. They cannot choose not to make supplies. Companies are obliged to make the tax deductions. HMRC might not have received payment from the next payroll, but the bill would have accrued anyway.

We should have gone to court and challenged their attempt to appoint their own administrators. However, Duff and Phelps negotiated with HMRC and said Rangers wouldn't object to their challenge as long as they were appointed as administrators.

This sounded like an acceptable compromise. I thought I was in control of the situation. I genuinely believed we could emerge a debt-free club, that I'd still be at the helm and we could move on.

If my short time at Rangers had taught me anything, however, it was that the moment I thought I was in command was precisely the time it all fell apart.

What I didn't realise is that those I thought were on my side appeared to be developing a more equivocal relationship with other parties.

The coming weeks and months would see Rangers taken to the edge of the precipice – and then plunged right over.

When the dust finally settled, both myself and HMRC would live to regret what happened next.

**EXCLUSIVE: A Scots billionaire is on the brink of buying Rangers. Talks with tycoon Craig White over a £30million takeover early next year are believed to be at an advanced stage**

In Monaco in the late 90s. That headline in the *Daily Record*, incorrectly stating that I was a billionaire, was unhelpful and misleading, creating unrealistic expectations in the eyes of some Rangers' supporters.

David Murray was keen to have a ceremonial signing for the cameras. In actual fact the deal had been signed the day before.

Once a season ticket holder, I was now back as owner of Rangers. *Press Association.*

Rangers fans greeting me on the way to my first game as owner. *Press Association*

Sitting with the old board at my first game as owner. They were all perfectly nice to my face that day but had done all they could to block my takeover bid. *Press Association*

My team with Donald Muir (far right), who passing on interesting information about Martin Bain. Sitting in the stand was the only place where we felt we could get any privacy. *SNSPix*

With the league trophy, secured, with victory away to Kilmarnock. The scenes at Ibrox afterwards will live with me forever. *SNSPix*

Unfurling the league flag before the opening game of the season. It was one of my better days at the club. *SNSPix*

I got on well with manager Ally McCoist, in the early days at least. *SNSPix*

The rise and fall of my time at Rangers, luridly captured by the tabloids.

David Whitehouse and Paul Clarke of Duff and Phelps taking over as administrators. *Getty Images*

Leaving court after one of the pre-trial hearings. *Getty Images*

Charles Green, who I caught on tape admitting shafting me, at court, with DCI Jim Robertson on the left of the picture. *Getty Images*

Exiting the High Court after being found not guilty by the jury. I was elated at winning the case, but the reason I was laughing was that I'd got stuck in the door with two cops – probably the worst time for that to happen, with dozens of photographers outside.

# THIRTEEN

BIGGART BAILLIE OFFICES, Glasgow, February 14, 2012

I was sitting in the lawyers' office with David Grier, Paul Clark and David Whitehouse of Duff and Phelps. They were explaining to me the development with HMRC that was allowing them to be administrators.

'This is great news,' I said. 'Well done.'

I looked around but my smile was not being returned. Paul Clark visibly tensed up. That was when I knew. They weren't on my side any more.

Suddenly I was on my own, exposed – a starring role in my very own St Valentine's Day massacre. I looked around at the stern faces staring back at me. There wasn't a lot of love in the room. For the first time since getting involved in this bizarre deal I had the feeling my own personal guarantee to Octopus was at risk. I had always believed that as long as there was a club called Rangers playing out of Ibrox with me in charge, the Ticketus investment was safe. Was I still going to be in charge?

If I'd known what was going to happen I would have tested HMRC's challenge to our notice period in court. Instead we capitulated – my thinking being that having Duff and Phelps in there would be better than any HMRC-appointed agents. As it was Duff and Phelps were as difficult for me as any firm HMRC could have appointed.

Now Duff and Phelps were acting with HMRC, anything could happen. And it did. That day, HMRC forced Rangers FC into administration. The situation was spinning out of my control.

HMRC put restrictions on Duff and Phelps, but basically they were happy for them to be the administrators. I had appealed the 'small tax case', the discounted option scheme liability. However, Duff and Phelps backed down and agreed with HMRC that they would accept that as a liability. This was, of course, the result HMRC wanted.

As MCR, I had brought them into this deal. I had considered David Grier, in particular, a friend. I now felt as though I was being frozen out.

If I'd got the month's notice, as I'd been advised, all the cash that was in the bank would have gone on salary payments and other things that had to be paid and there would be no money left for them to get their hands on. If that had happened they would have been forced to do things differently.

My opinion, later confirmed in legal documents, was that the very hard line of HMRC and the possibility of an uncapped fee placed them in a conflicted situation with regard to their allegiance to me. There would then be a potential upside to them from an HMRC driven administration in which they would very much be in the running to get the job. It wasn't a guarantee and they wouldn't have known for sure the club was going to go into administration. But in their line of business they knew it was probable they were going to get it.

Once Rangers went into administration, Duff and Phelps could dictate their own fees – that's what happens in these situations. The administrators collect any money that is due into the club. It can be from ticket sales, or player sales, or payments that are due in from the league, or TV money. The administrators then get paid before any of the creditors. The fees rack up very quickly when you have a number of people working there, all charging considerable hourly rates.

This isn't a particular criticism of Duff and Phelps. It happens with all insolvency practioners.

As we had inched towards administration there was always a fear at the back of my mind that this scenario might unfold. I had plenty of prior experience of dealing with that.

I wondered if part of the reason HMRC had refused to have that discussion about how to repay the liability was because Duff and Phelps effectively said they had to put the club into administration – it was the only way they were going to get their money.

We had gone to HMRC weeks earlier and proposed a CVA to them where all the creditors would get 100 pence in the pound over 18 months, with the exception of the 'big tax case' which wasn't settled then. Again HMRC refused.

Rangers eventually went into administration because of the outstanding VAT and PAYE. We had offered to pay that over six months between February and the transfer window closing in August. It totalled between £5-6 million and they refused that, too.

I'd never known anything like it. I'd been involved in lots of businesses and because of the nature of what I do, every business has a problem with HMRC. Every company I've been involved with has had PAYE arrears. As soon as a company's got problems, it's the first thing to go. No one can stop your supplies, employees can't walk out. Whatever your business, it's logical not to pay HMRC if the business is struggling for cash.

On pretty much every past occasion when I have gone to HMRC to discuss making payments over a period of time, they have agreed to it. They might negotiate on the payment terms. I've seen them give three-year payment terms, as long as the repayments are kept up-to-date.

What happened with Rangers was a first. I'd never known HMRC to say no to getting paid, because all they want to do is collect money. With Rangers, there was just no way.

Even then, it didn't make sense to push the club into administration. HMRC were never going to get all the money back. They were going to rack up millions on legal fees. They had a claim for £75-80 million by the time all penalties and interest were added on. When everything was accounted for, it would have been closer to £100 million. If they were lucky they might have got ten pence in the pound, or they might have got nothing. It just didn't make sense. They could have done a deal, but they don't think like a commercial organisation.

As soon as we served notice to appoint administrators, the media went haywire. 'Darkest Day at Ibrox' was one of the doomsday headlines, which seemed inappropriate when you considered the stadium disasters that weighed heavily on the club's history.

At Auchenhowie, I held a meeting with Ally McCoist, the players, the coaching staff and the other employees to try to bring them up to speed with the latest developments. I couldn't offer them any guarantees with regard to their long-term futures, but I did say I hoped I would still be running the football club if it entered administration, confirmed later that day by the actions of HMRC. Ali Russell and Gordon Smith were with me. Some of the players had questions. We did our best to answer them.

We held a similar meeting at the club canteen. Some of the staff had links to the club that stretched back 50 years. I could see the pain etched on their faces. It was fair to say there was a mixture of sadness, shock, disbelief and anger, aimed at David

Murray and myself. I had enormous sympathy for anyone who feared they were about to lose their job, but it looked like nobody would and any hardship was a consequence of solving a problem that was not of my making.

After those formalities, suddenly I was an outcast. Duff and Phelps were in charge, and they swiftly instructed everybody not to deal with me.

Nine months earlier I had been cheered into the main entrance of the Bill Struth Stand. Now, on a cold February evening, I stood outside that same door, flanked by police officers and to a barrage of boos delivered a statement trying to explain to fans what was happening to their club. I made it clear the problem remained with HMRC, whose reluctance to compromise had left us facing a bill that could top £75 million unless we took drastic action.

We were instantly handed a 10-point penalty, leaving us 14 behind leaders Celtic. Effectively that handed them the title, but it was one that would be won by default.

Celtic's Peter Lawwell, so keen to build alliances months earlier, was one of the first to kick us when we were down by stating his club didn't need Rangers – an opinion that was in stark contrast to the mood at the start of the season, when he wanted to know how we could work together to advance the departure of both clubs from the Scottish scene. They definitely do need each other – as events would soon prove.

David Murray announced his surprise that matters had got to this stage, Alastair Johnston demanded a police probe, while Paul Murray came forward to say he and a band of 'Blue Knights' were willing to save the club. At that stage, however, they were empty words as I, as majority shareholder, was still the only one who could get a CVA through.

Almost everybody that had come into contact with me at some stage in my life was approached for comment – my father-in-law waded in, as did the author of the book that first drew attention to my business success. A protest banner was pinned to the gates of Castle Grant. A lone voice amid the clamour was that of my sister, unfairly dragged into it, but stoically standing up for me.

The team had to prepare for a match against Kilmarnock. Ally McCoist made his soon to be famous 'We don't do walking away' statement. It wasn't something I wanted to do, either. I remembered, when I took over the club, doing an interview for STV and being asked, 'Are you the right guy for Rangers?'

I said I was the right guy at that particular time, because I thought I had the skill set required to sort out Rangers' problems. Even as events unfolded I still believed that to be the case, but matters were outside my control.

Ahead of the game there was a risk that the fans might cause a riot if I turned up. Reluctantly, I announced I was stepping aside to let the administrators do their job.

Amid the barrage of headlines, accusations and downright untruths, there was a bizarre moment of humour. One of the funniest headlines – and up there with the things you thought you'd never have to deal with – was a front page splash in *The Sun*: 'Craig Whyte's tax advisor is a porn star.'

The paper had discovered that Baxendale Walker not only produced his own porn films, he starred in them as well. As was the case with many stories, the part referring to me wasn't true. He wasn't my tax advisor – he had been David Murray's. But it was open season as far as I was concerned. The crazy thing was, the porn allegation was true. I spoke to the guy from *The Sun*. He said when they called Baxendale Walker they expected him to deny it but he said, no, he was a single guy, why not? In the brief encounter I had with him I had no idea he was a porn star.

That story aside, however, largely the coverage centred on missing millions.

Anyone reading the Scottish press would have come to the conclusion that I had pocketed all this unpaid tax and walked away with the money. That was the way it was presented. The media also said that I'd sold shares the club held in Arsenal and kept the proceeds – that was completely untrue. There was a lot of utter nonsense in the press. The average Rangers fan to this day probably still has the impression that I somehow robbed the club and took a load of money out of it. That wasn't true.

The people writing those stories were not experienced in business. They looked at some figures and thought, if the money's not there this guy must have taken it. The truth was, any money in the business was used as working capital to pay the bills and to keep the club going.

By that time nobody cared to come to me for any explanation – not even any right to reply. It was just a free for all. I retreated to Monaco, where it is illegal for paparazzi to take photographs, but they followed me there regardless. It was still generally a better place to be than in Scotland or London, but I was never away from the attention. Life became very intense.

I tried to deal with the hysterical reports. Certain sections of the media were engaging in a character assassination, but I remained confident that the administrators' report would prove that every penny that had come in and gone out of Rangers was properly accounted for.

It was important to state that I had not profited from Rangers personally since I became chairman and had paid all my expenses from my own funds. Johnston could call for his investigation, but I believed I had nothing to fear because any fair probe would prove that I had always acted in the best interests of Rangers and been involved in no criminal wrongdoing whatsoever.

I didn't want to become a distraction. Ally McCoist had a tough enough job as it was. Initially, I had been the lightning rod for the anger and the dismay. Before long I could see it was impacting on his ability to do his job. I formally stepped aside and announced that I would not remain as chairman following the restructuring. I even offered to gift some of the shares to a supporters' foundation in an effort to repair lost trust.

A lot was being made of the issue of not paying PAYE and VAT during my time in charge. But I tried to explain that it simply wasn't true to say that Rangers or I had reneged on paying those liabilities since the takeover. The truth was that around £4.4 million of the £9 million demand from HMRC was, in fact, the 'small tax case', including penalties, and which was still in dispute. We had offered to pay £2.5 million of the PAYE and VAT up front with the remainder at £500,000 a month – but HMRC had rejected that.

Given HMRC had clearly wanted to make an example of Rangers, I felt it would have been far too risky to pump further funds into the club while the result of the EBT tax case remained unresolved.

People needed to understand how crippling the 'big tax case' had been on Rangers' ability to operate. I rejected a claim that somehow I had speeded up the club's downfall to suit my own ends. 'Anyone who pretends that this has somehow been my goal is either a fool or has a particularly sharp axe to grind,' I said.

I tried to remind people that HMRC had frozen some of our bank accounts while we were in dispute. On top of that, we had other funds frozen because of legal claims by certain former members of the board, all of which contributed to the club falling into arrears on our monthly PAYE liabilities.

Administration had been looming over the club ever since the EBT issue raised its head. The club could not go on funding losses of up to £15 million a year. People seemed to forget that the previous board, under Alastair Johnston, had been talking seriously about administration two years earlier. If things had turned out differently with HMRC, I believed I had a plan that would have avoided administration and put Rangers back on a sound financial footing.

Some people came forward with offers to buy the club. My name had become so toxic I was open to all serious offers of outside investment. But the reality was that every one of them needed to have a final settlement of the 'big tax case' one way or another.

At a press conference, Paul Clark and David Whitehouse of Duff and Phelps stated that they were not working for me. They seemed to bristle at the suggestion. 'We act as officers of the Court and we are accountable to the Court,' they said. 'We have a statutory duty to act in the best interests of creditors and stakeholders and that is what we will do. The people who matter most are those who have the interests of Rangers very much at heart – the supporters, players and staff.'

They confirmed that money from Ticketus had been used to fund the deal, although they did also confirm the cash had been used to pay the £18 million debt to Lloyds Banking Group in May.

When that came out I was accused of being a liar. Even though there had been the issues of confidentiality surrounding Ticketus' involvement, I continued to regret not being completely open and upfront at the time of the takeover. It would have spared me much hurt – and would have given the fans clarity over what was happening.

I still believed the Ticketus deal was by far the best way to protect the club, because they had no security over any assets. The fans were also fully protected as it was me who gave Ticketus personal and corporate guarantees underwriting their investment.

What nobody seemed interested to hear was that it was me who was on the line for £27.5 million in guarantees and cash if the restructuring failed or was not allowed to proceed.

Instead people were lining up to take pot shots.

The SFA, in their wisdom, announced within weeks of Rangers going into administration that they deemed me 'not a fit and proper person' to be involved in a football club. Rangers were also charged with bringing the game into disrepute.

The declarations were made after a special meeting of the SFA board to hear the findings of an independent inquiry. They wanted a fall guy and that's what they got. The verdict was delivered by chief executive Stewart Regan, who I believe should have concentrated on getting his own house in order before casting aspersions on other organisations. In his eight years at the helm of the SFA he had presided over a series of controversies. By the time he stepped down in February 2018, Scotland had still failed to qualify for a major tournament, were without a manager after a botch up trying to find a replacement for Gordon Strachan, were without a long-term home stadium to play in and without a major sponsor.

They struck me as being completely clueless. They summoned me to attend a hearing in April, but there was absolutely no way I was going to play a part in their little charade. It was a farce. The SFA did not have the power to stop someone being a shareholder or in control of a Scottish football club. They could say I was not fit and proper all they liked. All it meant was that I couldn't have represented a club at an SFA council meeting and I couldn't go to the AGM. Big deal. It was a matter for Companies House who clubs had on their boards, not the SFA.

The SFA didn't stop there. At the subsequent hearing they banned me for life and fined me £200,000. It was a joke and I couldn't care less. It made no difference to my life whatsoever. I responded by saying, 'good luck collecting the money'. I didn't pay a penny of the fine and I never intend to.

When the revelations came out on the BBC about the disqualification, the SFA wrote to the club asking why I hadn't disclosed it. We wrote back explaining that under their rules it didn't have to be disclosed. The SFA then opened up an investigation into it.

When I met Regan in December I explained the club would most likely be entering administration. He said, 'Don't worry about it. You can still be involved. It's not a big deal.'

So what the SFA were saying privately beforehand was completely different from what they said in public.

It was the same with Doncaster and Ralph Topping, of the football league. I had dinner with Doncaster in October and told him administration was going to happen and again they were very supportive. He said the league was not a regulator, it was more of a trade body that was there to look after the interests of the various clubs and they would be supportive of anything I had to do.

They also slapped a 12-month signing embargo on Rangers and fined the club £160,000, which was extremely harsh and pretty pointless given the financial state they were in.

In fact, the move backfired. Duff and Phelps called it draconian. And when the names of the three members of the SFA's judicial panel leaked online there were threats from furious Rangers fans. Seven thousand supporters then marched on Hampden in protest against the sanctions.

The information coming from Duff and Phelps didn't help alleviate the concerns of the average fan. They claimed the club's debts could top £134 million and published a list of almost 300 separate creditors owed a total of £55 million. The potential tax debt was on top of that. It was claimed Rangers owed £2.3 million to 12 other football clubs, including Celtic, Palermo, Rapid Vienna, Manchester City and Arsenal, in transfer fees and wages for players taken on loan. Other creditors were said to be David Murray's group, G4S Security, all the way down to a face painting company that was apparently due £40.

But the amount Rangers owed the parent company I set up, the Rangers FC Group, was not clarified by Duff and Phelps.

The whole thing was toxic. Gary Withey resigned from Collyer Bristow, because of the accusations levelled at him and the law firm. Comments had been made in the press that were not true about failing to co-operate and the firm was receiving a number of calls and emails from very irate fans.

Withey did state that he hadn't had any concerns about me when we first met and said he was surprised how incredibly aggressive HMRC were towards the club and I.

'I could never work out why,' he said. It would be some time before either of us had clarity on that particular issue.

He expressed deep regret that he'd ever got involved with Rangers. It was becoming a common theme, and I could relate to it. David Murray came out once more to describe his regret at selling the club to me. It seemed further evidence of his concern about his legacy.

Murray proclaimed I had duped him, a statement that damaged me further in the eyes of the supporters. Murray also denied knowing anything of the Ticketus deal prior to selling the club. I had to bite my tongue. It would be many years before those words were challenged in a public forum.

As the battle for control of Rangers commenced, as many as 40 potential bidders came forward. Seven were considered credible in the eyes of the media and Duff and Phelps, but the only one I took seriously was that of Brian Kennedy, owner of the Sale Sharks rugby team.

Any potential bidder needed me because I was the majority

shareholder. Nobody else could agree CVA without me. Brian Kennedy came to visit me at Castle Grant and we had lunch together. I thought he was genuine in his offer. I could potentially have done a deal with him. But I told him I wouldn't do a deal if he joined forces with Paul Murray, which was his intention at the time. He assured me he would ditch him if I did a deal with him.

Other bidders were mentioned in the press but none of them ever spoke to me. Duff and Phelps tried with several different buyers, but they all walked away from it. There was a guy from Singapore, while an American, Bill Miller, was granted preferred-bidder status but withdrew his interest just four days later after being allegedly stunned at the torrent of email abuse he received. An advisor at his Club 9 Sports, said he was getting hundreds of emails every day, some saying, 'Go home Yank'.

It was my understanding, through third parties, that Miller's consortium wanted liquidation and at that point that was not going to be good for the club.

With so much focus on who would control the club, it was sometimes easy to forget that there was football still to be played. Despite all the distractions the team did manage to post some good results, but suffered a heavy loss at Celtic Park.

It was predictable that the Celtic fans would take the opportunity to rejoice in the misfortune of their rivals. One banner that didn't escape my notice proclaimed 'Craig Whyte, Celtic Legend'. That wasn't something I had imagined happening when I'd taken control of the club a year earlier.

I was a pariah, a crook, or a figure of fun. And at the same time I was expected to sit back while administrators that I had appointed carved up a club I had acquired fair and square.

Worse was to come.

Another ruling went against me. Duff and Phelps had applied for a court decision on the legality of the Ticketus arrangement

– to see whether they even had a claim on the season tickets. Lord Hodge declared the season ticket deal to be void. He said you couldn't sell a personal right in Scotland, and took a seat to be that right – therefore it couldn't be done. Any other club doing similar deals would have had to stop. I thought it was unfair to Ticketus and to me, but that appeared to be the law in Scotland and nobody had checked it out previously.

Rangers had used Ticketus several times before. It was very common. But Duff and Phelps wanted that judgment because without it the business would have been completely unsellable. It was a key development. If Lord Hodge had ruled that the Ticketus model was all fine, the only person who could have bought Rangers back was me. To get a CVA through – and if Ticketus were going to stay on board in any way, shape or form – there was only one person that could have owned it and that was me, because no one else would have taken on that liability. Ticketus would have still owned the tickets and we would have kept rolling over season ticket deals.

Ticketus was routinely portrayed in the media as a scam or underhand deal, using the fans' money to buy the club. I was portrayed as having done something illegal by using Ticketus as a financing method, whereas it was an established practice in football finance – look at how the Glazer family bought Manchester United. They acquired the club much more aggressively than I had. The difference, however, was that they were 100 per cent up front about how they were financing it, whereas I wasn't.

That legal development meant I was being frozen out of my own deal. I risked losing everything and potentially faced bankruptcy, as Ticketus prepared to sue me for their lost investment.

I needed to find a solution. Desperate times called for desperate measures.

An opportunity presented itself – a chance to get one over on all those who, in my opinion, had wronged me.

It was a last throw of the dice. But I now had nothing to lose.

# FOURTEEN

GROSVENOR HOUSE HOTEL, London, March 2012

The man in front of me seemed a bit of a nutter, but he talked a good game. Charles Green. A seemingly affable Yorkshire man with a background in football – not entirely successful. He could just be the man to help me win back control of a club being wrenched from my grasp.

I'd reached out to some contacts to help find me someone who might front a deal. Imran Ahmad, a city dealer I had dealt with years previously, suggested Charles Green. Ahmad set up a meeting at the Park Lane hotel and made the introduction. This was a high-risk strategy, with more than a reasonable chance of backfiring. But I was running out of options.

I explained the issues to Green: 'I can't get involved, but I need someone to do two things – one, raise some money and two, front up a deal. I will stay in the background.'

He nodded. He could do that.

Green had been chief executive of Sheffield United in the nineties. He floated the club on the stock exchange but stood down when the business ran up crippling debts. His sudden arrival on the scene was bound to cause suspicion, but he was worth a gamble.

With my business associate Aidan Earley, I bought a shelf company called Sevco 5088. The plan was that Green would front up an offer to Duff and Phelps. I appointed Green as a director of Sevco 5088, but he also signed a blank resignation form and two blank appointment forms, so I could appoint directors and remove him if I wanted to. Charles had no money, however, and wanted a loan for legal fees. So I agreed to lend him £250,000 and paid the first tranche of that into Ahmad's mother's account, to pay the deposit to Duff and Phelps.

I was gambling that Duff and Phelps would have to listen to Charles Green. With one preferred bidder falling by the way side, they too were running out of options. If they wanted their fees they needed a deal to go through. And for a CVA to happen, the successful bidder had to deal with me. So they still needed me. If I didn't cooperate, they had no CVA.

Would it have mattered if they had known it was me behind the deal? Probably not. Would they care? I don't think they had anything personal against me. They wanted to be friends with HMRC and HMRC might not have been too happy at my return. But Duff and Phelps didn't have to worry about their fees being capped at £500,000 any more, and they didn't have any other issues with me as far as I knew.

Having my name attached to any bid at this stage would have been damaging for everyone. The media had demonised me to such a degree that if the fans thought I was behind a new deal they might have boycotted season tickets. Certainly at that stage I didn't want it to become public knowledge that I was behind the scenes.

The SFA had banned me, but they couldn't stop me if I wanted to be involved. I was being blamed for everything, which I found terribly unfair. So this development amused me.

I deliver this front man, but it is really me behind the scenes all the time. That says 'fuck you' to all these people – the SFA, Duff and Phelps, everybody.

I went into Hakkasan restaurant in Mayfair and introduced Paul Clark to Charles Green. I took Charles Green to Ticketus. It was very funny.

Green's offer price was £7.5 million for the club if there was a CVA and £5.5 million for the assets alone if the CVA didn't go through. Duff and Phelps liked Charles Green and said to me he seemed like the real deal. They asked if I was definitely letting Charles Green have my shares.

'Subject to Charles doing what he needs to do,' I said, 'yes.'

Everybody was happy – including me. There was a chance it could work. Ticketus had already launched their legal action against me for the millions used to fund the deal. I had to do something.

By the time Duff and Phelps announced Charles Green's interest publicly in May 2012, they said he had a period of exclusivity to complete the purchase of the club. Green said he was fronting a consortium of unnamed backers. He said he had done a deal with me to buy my shares for £2 – a 100 per cent profit on my initial outlay, Green said. He never did pay the £2 or buy my shares in Rangers FC.

Duff and Phelps were briefing the media that the Green deal was nothing to do with me – and all the time I was telling Green and Ahmad what to say to Duff and Phelps.

People in the know knew I was lurking behind the scenes for a bit. They might not have known the details, but they knew there was something going on.

I had a drink with David Grier while they were doing the deal. He said to me, 'So you're still involved then?'

I just laughed.

'Good luck with that,' he said.

It was the same with Ally McCoist. He called me up and asked what was going on. What did I think about this guy Green? I just laughed. He twigged I was still involved.

A barrister acting for Aidan Earley told Paul Clark of Duff and Phelps that we'd got Charles Green's signed resignation letter and Clark put his head in his hands. They had probably asked Green and he must have said he wasn't fronting for me. Maybe they satisfied themselves. I don't think they cared. They had no other offers at that time.

They'd already tried a CVA with several different buyers and they'd all walked away from it. Brian Kennedy would have done it and he could have been a good owner for Rangers, but he needed me to make it happen. Once I knew Green was interested, I cooled my interest in working with Kennedy.

The fans seemed relieved that someone else had come forward – someone pledging to keep the club debt free. Green attended the last game of the season, a 4-0 win in Perth against St Johnstone, to the sound of applause from some of the supporters keen to give him a cautious welcome.

Duff and Phelps drafted a CVA to creditors, offering them less than 10 pence in the pound. Legal fees were disclosed as over £5 million, with their own fees expected to be over £3 million. The club had been in administration for one 107 days.

In a fresh BBC documentary, the same journalist who revealed my disqualification, Mark Daly, turned his attention to the other people involved in the deal. He put the spotlight on David Grier for being involved from the start. Grier was forced to deny he had known anything about the Ticketus involvement. Daly also revealed the £500,000 cap for administration fees I had insisted upon. Paul Clark defended Duff and Phelps' position in that regard, claiming it referred to information I had supplied to them for a specific administration outcome. 'This outcome did not materialise and therefore the quotation was redundant,' he said.

Surprisingly, even though Duff and Phelps were publicly denouncing me, David Grier still seemed to think of me as their mate. On May 31, 2012, after the BBC documentary, Grier met me in Home House private members' club in Marylebone, London, near to their office in Portland Square. My aim was to get something to use in my defence. They had been briefing against me and had not been honest in public. They could have said they knew about Ticketus, but instead they stoked the flames. So I recorded the conversation in the hope he would confirm knowing about Ticketus.

We talked about how events had transpired. Grier wanted me to say publicly that Duff and Phelps did not know the full extent of the Ticketus finance. He was asking me to say he didn't know about it. They knew about Ticketus being a funder, but they were not part of the Ticketus financing arrangements, he said. This is useful, I thought. There were all sorts of other admissions, indiscreet things that I never imagined would ever become public.

On June 12, 2012, at a meeting at Ibrox, the Green CVA was tabled before creditors. Ahead of the meeting Dave King urged a boycott of season tickets and told creditors to reject the CVA. Thirty creditors were represented at the meeting, but the CVA failed because HMRC voted it down and as they represented more than 25 per cent of the creditors, that was enough to reject it. The club was therefore liquidated – 140 years of history wiped out in eight minutes. HMRC's reasoning was that by rejecting the CVA they could have a fuller investigation into the running of the company. They wanted to pursue the EBT debt and didn't want to accept a final settlement on that. They accepted a lower amount than they could have got if they had gone for the CVA. It was a decision they would come to regret.

David Grier told me one of the reasons HMRC gave, privately, for turning down the CVA proposal was that Dave King had gone public advising creditors to vote against the CVA. This meant Dave King helped kill the old Rangers, as it were.

BDO were appointed as liquidators. Green was now able to pay £5.5 million for the company's assets – Ibrox Stadium, Murray Park and the Albion car park – and they were to be transferred into the new company, which I believed was Sevco 5088.

Duff and Phelps had announced that I stood to gain nothing from the liquidation as they had not considered me a viable creditor.

However, in the wider business community it was general knowledge that I was still involved. The businessman Willie Haughey called me, saying he was representing Walter Smith. 'We want to take your deal out,' he said.

If I did a deal with Walter that sorted out the fans, Willie said, referring to the threat of a season ticket boycott. 'The fans don't like Charles Green, or they think he's fronting for you,' he added.

'£20 million and you can have it,' I said to Willie.

'No,' he replied. 'We'll only pay what you paid for it.'

They wanted to buy it for £5 million. I thought it was a cheeky offer. They were just trying to take advantage of a situation where the fans weren't buying season tickets. If they wanted to buy the club they would have to pay a premium.

Another person to approach me was Jim McColl, of Clyde Blowers engineering company. He was well-known in Rangers' circles. He was also one of my neighbours in Monaco. We shared the same housekeeper. Everyone wanted him to buy the club because he was mega rich. He didn't offer anything, however. The media kept talking about him as a potential saviour because he was supposedly a billionaire. He invited me for dinner in Monaco and he told me all the reasons why he would be interested in buying it. However, his investors in his engineering business wouldn't let him do it, so I was left wondering why he had invited me for dinner. He was a nice guy but he couldn't do anything.

Various weird and wonderful people wanted to buy the club at some stage. Somebody who claimed to be representing the Russian oligarch Boris Berezovsky said he was interested. He wanted to put money into it and compete with Chelsea because he didn't like Roman Abramovich. How seriously can you take that sort of thing? Probably not very.

In July, the SPL clubs voted not to allow the new Rangers into the top league. A week later, the football league clubs blocked a bid for the club to start its new life in the First Division, opting instead to order Sevco Rangers to begin its reincarnation in the bottom tier, the Third Division.

I never thought it would come to that. It was absurd. I'm sure the directors of the other clubs would not have wanted that to happen – it was completely down to fan power. All the fans of the other clubs threatened not to buy season tickets, as I understood it, if the new Rangers were admitted to the SPL. I understood the anger at the time, but I was surprised that the league and the clubs allowed it to happen. It put a huge financial strain on the other clubs and made Scotland a laughing stock on the world stage. What other country would penalise one of its leading clubs so severely?

The first game of the new season on July 29 saw Rangers away at Brechin City in the Challenge Cup. Jim Park, the cousin of Douglas Park and a businessman who I had put in place to help Green find investors, chauffeured Green to Brechin in my car. I interviewed the new finance director along with Imran Ahmad sometime in August. I thought I knew everything that was going on.

Unbeknown to me, however, Charles Green had set up another company called Sevco Scotland Ltd and transferred the rights from Sevco 5088 to it. Once he had the assets, Sevco Scotland Ltd changed its name to The Rangers Football Club, as it stands now. He was supposed to keep me informed of everything that was going on, but he didn't.

He had announced to the press that Sevco 5088, which was my company, had bought the assets. All of a sudden he changed it and announced it would be Sevco Scotland Ltd. I called him and asked what was going on. He waffled and said nothing had changed, but it clearly had.

I spoke to Green and Ahmad a few times. They still needed me to do things for them. For instance they needed me to agree to change the name of the old company. When I spoke to Green about the name change I recorded the conversation. I don't ordinarily record conversations, but I had cause to do it with people I didn't trust. First Grier, and now Green.

'Don't worry Craig,' Charles said. 'I'll look after your interests. You are Sevco.'

He might have talked a good game, but I still didn't trust him. This, after all, was a man who described himself in public as a 'nutcase'.

I felt I was being strung along.

I was sick of being blamed for creating the mess around Rangers and now people were airbrushing history.

It seemed unfair that I was the guy in the frame, taking the heat for the downfall of Rangers when the problems had been caused by the previous board and by David Murray in particular.

By the same token, I couldn't blame anyone other than myself. It was completely my own fault. I could have walked away from the deal. Although I thought had been treated unfairly, I could have handled things better. I felt it was important to set the record straight and get the facts out there.

I sat down with Chris McLaughlin, the BBC reporter who had spoken to me outside Ibrox on that first day. That seemed like a distant memory now.

It was by no means a soft-soap interview. He put it to me that I had lied about the Ticketus involvement. I denied that, but admitted I might have misled fans. I regretted not being more open. I said that everyone on my side – including Duff and Phelps – knew about Ticketus. And I stated that Murray and the board, while not being in full knowledge of what was going on, knew third-party funds were being used.

I also said for the first time publicly that I had brought Charles Green's consortium to the table and introduced him to Duff and Phelps.

Perhaps predictably, both Charles Green and Duff and Phelps denied my claims. Green said it was 'misleading' to suggest I'd brought them in, while Duff and Phelps branded the accusations 'malicious and without foundation'.

I knew not to expect any sympathy from the media, some of which had me pegged as the bad guy from the outset. The *Daily Record* kept up its relentlessly negative campaign against me. I was in a supermarket with my daughters, who at the time were 10 and seven. They came up to me with a copy of the *Record* saying, 'Look, there's daddy with a funny nose.'

The paper had done me up with a Pinocchio nose. I said: 'Come on girls, let's get out of here.'

That was the sort of shit I had to put up with. I was telling the truth, but the *Daily Record* was accusing me of being a liar.

While still at Rangers, I had put out a press release basically telling the fans not to read the *Record* because it was shit. So this was them getting their revenge. They found a picture of me aged nine or 10 in a football team in Scotland – I don't know how they got it – and said at least there's one football team he didn't fuck up.

I wasn't sure what I'd done to deserve such treatment. I don't think I told any direct untruths to the media. There were maybe things I didn't tell them, but I didn't blatantly lie about anything.

Another ridiculous *Daily Record* story a few months later was that I'd gone to Tesco in Inverness and a group of people had been thrown out for shouting 'a tirade of abuse' at me. It was total fiction. They did get a picture of me at the checkout with my shopping. I was a normal guy trying to live a normal life. Was I not allowed to go to the supermarket? Hollywood film stars can go to the supermarket without getting harassed but at that time I couldn't. They were forced to print a retraction and apology – they admitted there had been no tirade of abuse and nobody had been thrown out.

People were so entrenched in their positions that putting my side across didn't have that much of an impact. I had no PR company to fall back on. After the administration, both Media House and Hay McKerron bailed after a couple of weeks. When you have problems, you find out who your real friends are. A lot of people ditch you. It would have been useful if they had continued acting for me, but they made some excuse for not representing me. 'We're not really sure what we can do for you anymore until you know what your strategy is going forward, so we think it would be best...'

Media House only looked after me in my capacity with Rangers, yet within two years of administration they too would have their ties to the club cut.

I suspected people like David Murray and members of the old board were still manipulating their media contacts by briefing against me. I thought that was unfair, but not necessarily unexpected in the circumstances. However, the onslaught of media abuse was never-ending. I was surprised at just how nasty it was. It was horrible because everybody you've ever known sees it, but you just have to keep going.

It put me off flying back to Scotland. I still had the place at Grantown, but I ended up not using it. I didn't want to go to Scotland because of all the aggravation. Going up in the train was like entering a different universe. In London or Monaco no one knew who the hell I was and that was the way I liked it. Suddenly I went to Scotland and almost as soon as I crossed the border I had people coming up to me. As someone who had spent nearly his entire career being anonymous it was very discomforting.

I was the subject of several death threats, mostly online, people saying they'd happily take a life sentence to do me in. Another threatened to fire bomb the castle. Thankfully, the only actual instance of aggravation I had encountered had come in Monaco in May at the grand prix. An angry fan pulled me up while I was sitting in the Cafe De Paris and started grilling me about my time at Rangers, but I told him that history will judge me differently.

I would have to accept that, for a good while at least, Celtic fans would consider me a hero, while Rangers supporters hated me. The obscenely biased media coverage hadn't helped in that regard.

Charles Green and Ahmad were planning a stock floatation around December 2012. They kept me dangling until the floatation. I could have stopped it happening by making the evidence I had public then. They got me to do a couple of other things for them, but after they got everything they needed they basically told me where to go.

They were shafting me. The new Rangers club acquired those assets by transferring them from Sevco 5088, fraudulently, in my opinion.

I had never known a deal like this one. Ever since I'd got

involved with Rangers I'd never had so many people try to shaft me.

I realised they were reneging on our deal, so I tried to make things easy for them.

'Pay me some money,' I said, 'and I'll go away and forget all this happened. I'll keep all your secrets and it will never come out that I was involved.'

How much was I after they asked?

'Give me a million quid.'

They offered me half a million.

'I'm not doing that,' I said.

Charles Green stopped taking my calls. Imran Ahmad effectively said too bad, we'll sort you out, don't worry.

For a while they kept waffling, 'we're going to pay you, we're going to pay you'. I was open to doing a deal, but of course they never did. I realised they never going to settle.

You feel betrayed when somebody is sitting over lunch with you in London saying, 'Don't worry, Craig, I'll look after your interests.'

I suspected at the time I might not be able to trust the guy. Green had been a last resort. He was the only option around given the time constraints and given that nobody else wanted to buy the club and given I couldn't do it myself because of the publicity and the pressure from the SFA. If Green had not bought it I don't know what we could have done. Brian Kennedy was probably the only alternative option. In hindsight he might have been the better prospect, both for me and for Rangers.

I thought Green wouldn't be stupid enough to double cross me. But he did.

I thought he was intelligent enough to realise it was a bad idea to fall out with me, because he signed the blank director forms and the blank share transfer forms. I thought given that he's done that, given he's had the publicity of taking over a football club surely he's not going to be stupid enough to shaft me. But he was.

As for Ahmad, his actions didn't surprise me. He was like a lot of city types – out to make a fast buck.

Even if the plan had worked, I would probably have had to stay in the background for quite some time. Given the vitriol from sections of the media, it would have been extremely difficult to sell the idea that I was still calling the shots to the fans.

But I couldn't just sit back and watch Green and Ahmad get away with what I viewed as a blatant fraud. I had to do something. I began plotting my revenge.

# FIFTEEN

FOR ONCE IT was a tabloid paper I was happy to buy. The front page headline proclaimed: 'Green: I Shafted Whyte to Get Gers.'

The *Scottish Sun* was relatively friendly and didn't have the same agenda as some of the others. When I decided to go public over Charles Green's double cross, they were the logical choice. I let them hear the tapes of our conversations.

Green tried to claim he had only been telling me what I wanted to hear so he could get his hands on my shares. But he basically admitted he defrauded me and the other investors in Sevco 5088. When *The Sun* confronted him with the story he said, 'What we had to do at the start was get the confidence of this guy for him to give us the shares, to give us the debentures, to do a whole raft of things . . . We kept him sweet to prise the club from him.' Green then unilaterally decided to move the deal.

I'd given him an out. I'd said I would walk away for a million quid and 25 per cent of his and Ahmad's shares. If he had done that deal none of this would have come out in public and he would still be there, most likely. He was a silly guy.

Green had reportedly raised £22 million from his share issue, but two weeks on from the revelations he stepped down as chief executive, just 340 days after assuming control. He continued to deny any wrongdoing, but Rangers had announced an independent inquiry into his takeover. A few days later, Ahmad also quit.

Within months of the share issue, the money had reportedly gone. Incredibly, Green managed to walk away with £933,000, which angered the fans. It didn't have to be that way.

After doing what I felt I had to in order to settle the score, I tried to keep my head down in Monaco and I attempted to get on with my life. It wasn't easy. And it was going to get a hell of a lot worse before it got better. It was a deeply challenging time.

My marital dispute with Kim had spilled into court with the arrest and subsequent conviction of two former housekeepers relating to the theft of items from Castle Grant.

I had Ticketus pursuing me over their lost millions. Technically it was not their money they'd lost. And they had actually lost the money because of bad legal advice. If anyone had bothered to check out if the deal worked under Scottish law it wouldn't have happened in the first place. Had Ticketus known that advance sales of season tickets would not be legal in Scotland, or not enforceable in Scotland, they would never have done the deal and I would never have signed the personal guarantee.

I signed the personal guarantee on the basis that when I bought Rangers I knew administration, liquidation or resale was a distinct possibility. However, given Rangers had been using Ticketus as a financing model before, I never imagined a scenario coming to pass where Ticketus wouldn't be able to own the seats.

I didn't want to become bankrupt. Anyone active in business who thinks they might be sued has protective measures in place and I've always had that to a certain extent – but it was inevitable I would lose Castle Grant, especially after my wife rejected my plan for it. We owned it jointly and, even though it had become a bit of an albatross, I had asked my wife to transfer her shares in the castle to me. She refused. After that, I thought it pointless to lay out any more money on it. My intention had been to transfer the shares into a trust for the children's benefit. One of us should have gained from the place. It was unfortunate, however, how things had developed.

I wasn't particularly hung up on keeping a castle in Scotland as a single guy. What did I need a 70-room house for?

For what it was worth I attempted to fight the bankruptcy, but I was in danger of losing everything I had worked hard to build up in the last few years.

Another consequence of the Rangers fiasco was that Merchant was liquidated. I never had been regulated when I was involved with financial services, but I wasn't involved in that line of business any more, largely because Rangers took up so much of my time that I was unable to concentrate properly on my other business.

Since getting involved with Rangers, I'd experienced some bizarre and disturbing moments. Yet nothing prepared me for the violation I felt in May 2013 when a hacker accessed my emails and tried to blackmail me to stop them being leaked.

The hacker William Stevenson was believed to be a Celtic fan, based in Manchester. He sent me some threatening emails demanding I send him a copy of what Celtic fans called 'the five-way agreement', the document that set out the terms of Sevco Scotland Ltd's takover of The Rangers Football Club Plc, the company I set up that had gone into administration, which was signed off by the SPL, the SFA and the Scottish Football League. I didn't have a copy of the agreement. He didn't believe me. If I didn't send him a copy he was going to release the material he had hacked publicly.

I responded to a couple of his emails. He tried to say various things to blackmail me. Then he tried to sell them back to me for £20,000. I declined.

Material started to appear on Twitter under the account @Charlottefakes. Murray had called my original takeover Project Charlotte as his office was in Charlotte Square in Edinburgh. The hacker quickly built up quite a following.

In some ways what he leaked wasn't that bad for me, because it was coming directly from my emails. As horrible as it was for that to happen, because it was private stuff that you don't want anyone to see, the stuff coming out was generally in my favour because I had done nothing wrong. I wasn't the only person he managed to hack. Several other people were victims. It was more embarrassing for Jack Irvine, Duff and Phelps and others.

Among the things he uncovered were recorded conversations with Duff and Phelps. I'd sent them to Gary Withey by email. On these recordings were indiscreet revelations about their personal lives. It was highly embarrassing, weird stuff that all became public.

David Grier later confronted me about it. I don't know how he tracked me down, but he found me in a hotel in Mayfair. He was very angry when he came up to me. He was, perhaps understandably, annoyed about the conversation I recorded and the circumstances surrounding the leaking of that meeting. He thought I had caused it to be made public, but it was the hacker.

We had a forceful conversation that day.

'You tried to fuck me over, David,' I said.

'No, I didn't,' he responded. 'I was trying to get a CVA through for you.'

That wasn't how it had looked at the time.

When things had calmed down between us, he did disclose that the police were giving them all a load of grief. A sign of what was to come, perhaps?

The hacker obviously managed to get in touch with Dave King, who at the time was mounting a comeback bid to be involved again at Ibrox. King paid the hacker £20,000 for the stolen data through a third party.

I complained to the Metropolitan Police as I believed, naively as it would transpire, that the normal rules of justice would apply to me. The Metropolitan Police passed it to Police Scotland, who had already begun an investigation into the goings on at Rangers. They arrested the hacker, but the Crown Office had other plans, as I would soon find out.

I was threatened with jail over the Ticketus case, but the simple matter was their lawyers had been having trouble serving court papers on me because I was out of the country.

If I thought that was unfair, however, it was nothing compared to what was coming.

There was something to be said for staying away from the UK, which for the most part of 2014 was what I did. Going from school into business, then marriage and family life, I'd never dedicated any time to travel. Now I had some time on my hands and I decided to take an extended break, explore parts of the world I hadn't had the chance to, and seek out some new business opportunities.

I was in Japan when a detective inspector called Jim Robertson tried to contact me. I ignored his call and talked to my lawyers instead. The police had been to see my lawyer Paul Kavanagh at his office in Glasgow.

'We want to arrest your client,' Robertson told Paul.

As well as me, they were going to arrest the Duff and Phelps three and Gary Withey. Their plan was to detain us, keep us in cells overnight and present us in court the following day. Given the passage of time from the perceived offences, it seemed unfair treatment. They would never do that in normal circumstances.

I asked Paul if he could sort it with the Crown Office so I could stay in a hotel for the night and I'd agree to attend a police station by appointment. They could arrest me and take me to court. I didn't see why I should spend the night in a police cell when I didn't have to.

The initial crown prosecutor, Jim Keegan, agreed to that. But then he had a discussion with the Lord Advocate Frank Mulholland and came back to say the deal was off. 'He'll have to spend the night in a police cell.'

Okay then, I thought, I'm not going to rush back. I was in Japan. There was no extradition treaty.

I thought I had the upper hand. I said I would come back when I did not have to spend the night in a police cell. It was perhaps a trivial point. I was prepared to go to court, but I wanted to be treated normally. I suspected they just wanted their marquee arrest in front of the cameras.

If they didn't want to agree, I was in Japan so there was nothing they could do.

I waited to see what would happen. I'm glad I did.

Early one Friday morning in November, over two and a half years after Rangers entered administration, police carried out raids on the homes of David Grier, David Whitehouse, Paul Clark and Gary Withey, detaining all four.

The timing was not accidental. After arresting the Duff and Phelps lot, the police drove them up the M6 and held them in a cell for the whole weekend, before their appearance in court on Monday. I must admit I did have a slight chuckle when I heard that. I'm sure it wasn't much fun for them.

When they appeared at Glasgow Sheriff Court that Monday they were confronted by fans who chanted 'scumbags'. It was apparently chaotic.

The prosecutors claimed that I tricked three companies into handing over more than £22 million – then told Sir David

Murray, the Rangers board and Lloyds banking group that the money was mine. I was said to have had another £4 million put into a client account held by London lawyers Collyer Bristow. It was further claimed I pledged Rangers a £9.5 million spending pot, but failed to pay tax and took the club into administration. I was also accused of lying to Ticketus and the SFA about the directorship ban.

David Grier was said to have told the Rangers directors I had enough cash to run the club back in 2011. Withey was accused of providing legal papers to say the money was mine. Prosecutors additionally claimed Clark and Whitehouse attempted to pervert the course of justice by telling police they didn't know about Ticketus.

A separate police investigation was looking at Charles Green's takeover. And a second warrant for my arrest was issued in England over the Ticketus case.

I definitely was in no rush to get back. I booked some further travel as I had no idea what was happening with the Crown Office.

The prosecutor kept talking to Paul Kavanagh and eventually they did agree that I could come back and go straight to court. The date we agreed was December 9. I said I had some business to take care of in the United States and Mexico, after which I would get a flight from Miami and return to the UK. I figured that after I was arrested I wouldn't have a passport, so I wanted two weeks to finish the things I was doing.

They agreed to this.

Fine, I thought. I would come back to face the music, but at least it was happening on my terms. I was the only person who knew my travel plans. I still had the upper hand.

Or so I thought.

# SIXTEEN

MEXICO CITY AIRPORT, November 26, 2014

'Ladies and gentlemen, we are commencing our descent.'

The flight from Japan to Mexico had been uneventful. I started to pack away my things. Once settled at a hotel in Mexico City, my intention was to spend a few days exploring some business opportunities, then on to Miami, to London and finally to Glasgow.

We landed and began taxiing to the terminal. There was another announcement: 'Ladies and gentlemen, as you disembark this aircraft, could you have your passports ready please. Police are carrying out an inspection.'

I froze. This meant only one thing. They were here for me.

There were two Mexican police officers. As soon as one checked my passport my fear was confirmed. In broken English, he explained: 'You are Craig Whyte? Come with us. This is probably a mistake – something to do with a football club in Scotland.'

They led me to a holding room and explained Interpol had instructed them to detain me. Clearly the Scottish police were more on the ball than I'd thought.

'We can't allow you to go into Mexico. You have two choices. Either we can put you on a flight back to Japan. Or you can fly to London.'

They were almost apologetic for detaining me. This wasn't an arrest, they said. The choice was mine. The thought of going back to Japan was very tempting. I could hide out there. What would they do then?

To hell with it, though.

'Put me on the flight to London.'

The cops were obviously determined to get me for something. It was time to go back and deal with it.

They took me to a holding room with several other people that weren't being allowed in to the country. We all looked at one another, each no doubt thinking, 'what have you done?'

I must be a rarity, I thought – a Brit being deported from Mexico.

The Mexican police were polite throughout. They paid for my flight to Heathrow. I was allowed access to my suitcase, so I looked out a suit and changed from my casual clothes. If the Glasgow cops wanted their grandstand arrest, I better look the part. No one would be escorting me from Mexico. No doubt the police would meet me on arrival at Heathrow.

I could only imagine what awaited me. Would I get to speak to a lawyer at any point, or would they whisk me straight to Barlinnie Prison, where I'd languish for months until my trial? Given everything else that had happened since I'd got involved with Rangers, I couldn't rule anything out. I was stepping into the unknown. I had no idea what was going to happen. Only that it was going to be bad.

For a moment, during the flight, I wondered whether there was a chance the police would be so disorganised they might miss me. Perhaps I could sail through passport control as normal.

That thought vanished the moment I saw two uniformed police officers stepping onto the plane. I was right at the back and their slow march up the aisle seemed to take an eternity.

'Craig Whyte? You're coming with us.'

Hauled off a plane, right in front of everybody. That's got to be one of life's most embarrassing moments.

Three more police officers waited to greet me off the plane. One tall man with a beard and moustache and a slim blonde woman introduced themselves as Detective Inspector Jim Robertson and his colleague Jacqui O'Neill. They seemed excited to see me. I wondered if this was a big moment for them.

'Craig Whyte. You're under arrest.'

I wondered how long DI Robertson had been waiting to say those words. The formalities over, they escorted me through passport control. No queues for detained fugitives. Then it was into a police van to switch terminals for the connecting flight to Glasgow. Once on board, we sat at the back of the plane. I was relieved there were no cuffs. This was a ridiculous enough situation already.

I was surprised at how chatty the police were. Robertson told me what a Rangers fan he was. He'd been enjoying investigating this case, meeting all his Rangers heroes.

'When this is all over,' he said, smiling, 'maybe we could go for a drink together.'

Bizarre doesn't even come close.

They had it all arranged so from the moment we touched down and came to a standstill there was transport all the way from the runway to the police station at Mount Florida. All of this for me. I was a special case. It hadn't needed to be like this. I would have turned up for questioning, appeared in court on an agreed date. They were obviously desperate to take me to court in a van.

We arrived at Mount Florida, coincidentally the one closest to Hampden Park, the home of Scottish football. My fear, as the only one charged with any offence in connection with the Rangers inquiry, was how far they would go to make an example of me. Robertson's admission of his allegiance confirmed my suspicions. The police was full of Rangers fans. They were desperate for so-called justice to be seen to be done, regardless of whether they found evidence of wrongdoing or not.

Before I was put in the cell I finally got my phone call. I spoke to Paul Kavanagh. The night in the cell I'd accepted. What worried me was not getting bail and being held in prison.

'Don't worry, you'll definitely get bail,' he said. That eased my mind.

When I finally saw the inside of the cell it wasn't as bad as I'd feared. I had a blanket and some water. They let me read my book and although it was hardly five-star accommodation I was so tired I actually dozed off. I might have been able to get a full night's rest, but an officer appeared on the hour every hour to make sure I hadn't topped myself.

In the morning they cuffed me for the transfer to the Sheriff Court, where I was held in a cell in the bowels of the building until my appearance before the judge. Within seconds I started pining for the police cell. It was bloody horrible, just a urinal and a thin wooden bench not big enough to lie on. I wasn't allowed my book. All I could do was read the graffiti on the walls. Thankfully there was nothing about me on there.

I was still in the same suit I'd travelled in and I sat there for eight hours. Eventually Paul appeared and I was allowed out of the cell to speak to him. A guard helpfully told me the police were warning that even if I was granted bail they were to arrest me for the outstanding warrant in England. As I'd been out of the country I hadn't appeared in court and the judge found me in contempt and had given me a four-week prison sentence. Could the day get any worse?

I'm never getting out, I thought. These guys are really out to get me. If they can find a way to keep me locked up, they'll do it.

Paul dismissed those fears in a second: 'The police don't have the powers to arrest you. It was an English civil case, not criminal.'

The hearing lasted about 20 minutes. As the police hadn't been allowed to interview me on my arrest, the prosecutor, or procurator fiscal, now asked me questions on their behalf.

My answer to every one was the same: 'On the advice of my solicitor I have no comment to make.'

Then came the words I'd been waiting on all day. The sheriff granted me bail. I'd been seeing a woman called Charlotte before my travels. We'd met at the Monaco grand prix and she had kindly given me her mother's home to use as a bail address as I didn't have anywhere in the UK to live. She lived in Lancashire. The police said they would drive me south.

'Don't trust the cops,' Paul said as I prepared to leave. 'Don't let them drive you into England just in case they do something with that other warrant.'

As I left the court a small group of fans hurled some abuse. It was so quick I couldn't catch much of what was said. It was to be expected. Given what had been said in the media, it was understandable that people would think I was the bad guy.

Charlotte headed north of the border and the police agreed to drop me at a service station on the M74 motorway, several miles before we reached England. I wasn't taking any chances. On the way down the road, DI Robertson seemed more interested in checking himself out on TV. He replayed the television coverage of my appearance at court, showing him by my side.

What baffled and infuriated me was that he was calling the lawyer acting for Ticketus, the other party in the English court case. They were like best buddies. How cosy that Police Scotland was cooperating so fully with an English lawyer in a civil matter.

By the time we reached the services and Charlotte greeted me, the exhaustion of three days on the go finally caught up with me. Relieved to be away from the police, I nearly collapsed when we reached her house.

I had survived the most traumatic day of my life. However, although I could relax, the relief was only temporary. I had to go to London the following week to appear in court over the civil case and the small matter of being sued for the £20 million I'd guaranteed.

There was a real danger I could go to prison over that.

I sunk into the sofa trying to process why I – and not the number of crooks who'd profited from the demise of a once proud institution – was the scapegoat.

I drifted into a fitful sleep.

The nightmare was just beginning.

# SEVENTEEN

ONLY IN GLASGOW.

The Lord Advocate, Frank Mullholland, while lapping up hospitality at Celtic Park following the arrest and charging of five people in connection with a takeover of Rangers, told the company how confident he was that, if the Crown got us all in front of a jury, we would definitely be found guilty.

That was what I was told. It was totally inappropriate. This was the same Lord Advocate who had ordered the investigation, apparently.

As far as I was aware there was no evidence of wrongdoing. It was shaping to be the kind of case where the prosecutors have a guy they think has done something wrong and find a crime to stick on him.

Again, only in Glasgow could you have the main investigating officer openly admitting to being a Rangers fan. I heard a rumour that the 'The Billy Boys' was sung to certain witnesses.

I still did not know why they would arrest me. I knew I had taken legal advice all the way through. I hadn't taken any money. It's not as if I had transferred money to an offshore account and I was now thinking, 'bloody hell this is going to be a big problem'.

There was nothing like that.

I hadn't taken a penny out of that club. I'd taken legal advice from people who I thought were competent professionals all the way through, so I had no idea what I was supposed to have done wrong. But this was Glasgow. This was Scotland. The tail wags the dog. Somebody had to be blamed for something. Somebody had to pay.

And, boy, were they trying to get something to stick on me.

My immediate concern was the threat of jail over the non-appearance in court in London, for the Ticketus case. I had been worrying about it, but I needn't have. The judge could have sent me to prison, but given I had surrendered myself to court that wasn't going to happen.

I stayed at Charlotte's place for a couple of weeks in Lancashire and then moved to the flat in Belgravia, London. My bail address was Charlotte's mother's house and as part of my bail conditions I had to sign at a police station up in Lancashire every week. It seemed like the waste of one day every week to do that and it went on for more than a year. It was completely pointless. I put up with the inconvenience because I didn't want to tell the Crown where I was living. My address had been leaked to the press previously and I didn't want it happening again. I was also under no obligation to give them my address. As it was, I would have been travelling north to meet my lawyer each week, so we arranged that he would come and meet me in Preston while I was there.

I would have my legal meeting and go through whatever stuff they came up with and then go and sign on at the police station. And back to London again.

I would have preferred to keep a low profile at this stage, but I felt pressurised into doing an interview with *The Sun* when they basically blackmailed me. They had been camped outside Charlotte's mother's house and got a picture of my girlfriend. I said I'd speak to them as long as they didn't run it, because she was unhappy. It wasn't fair on her to get dragged into it, because she had been kind to me during the arrest period.

I told them I was confident that I would clear my name. I said the prospect of jail wasn't nice to think about, but it didn't frighten me. I believed that. There was no point in worrying about things I couldn't control. It was a philosophy that would be seriously tested in the months ahead.

At Rangers, some of the people who had wanted control before I took over finally got their wish and seized the club. Dave King and Paul Murray assumed control after a turbulent couple of years since Green had been forced to stand down. By spring 2015 Ally McCoist had paid the price for failing to return the club to the Premiership, losing the Championship title to Hearts.

McCoist had been under pressure as Rangers manager during season 2014/15 as they fell behind Hearts in the race for the Championship title, and automatic promotion to the Premier League. In December 2014 he had given 12-months notice of his intention to resign, and was placed on gardening leave later that month.

King and Murray were deemed to be fit and proper persons in the eyes of the SFA, which had changed the wording of its questionnaire since I had completed it. I took that to be an admission that they were wrong in their assessment of whether I had lied or been misleading. My lawyer even advised them on the wording. They changed it to what he suggested. 'Have you served a ban within the last five years?'

Surely if their test had been foolproof there would have been no need to alter it?

Former Celtic star Davie Provan said King, on being accepted by SFA, had 'got a result that would make OJ Simpson blush.'

When I was arrested the police had searched my luggage and seized my laptop, two phones and an iPad. Nearly a year later they turned up at Charlotte's mother's house. I wasn't there because I wasn't living there. They accused her of covering for me, saying I'd clearly gone abroad, really giving her a hard time. She politely pointed out to them that, as they'd taken my passport from me, I might have struggled to leave the country.

'Oh, he can have another passport,' the cop replied.

My lawyer then got a call from the police threatening to revoke my bail conditions because I wasn't cooperating with them.

All this because they realised they couldn't get into any of my devices. They were all encrypted and sadly for them I'd forgotten all the passwords. They hadn't thought to ask for them until months later.

At the same time as they were hassling an older woman, insisting I had fled the country, I was sitting in Yates Wine Lodge in Preston, with Paul Kavanagh.

We told the police: 'Come and see us here if you want to talk to us.'

An officer from Police Scotland showed up and started reading me my rights.

Paul asked: 'What jurisdiction do you have to operate in England?'

'None, actually,' he said.

He asked for the passwords for the devices. He actually admitted the police had forgotten to ask me for them at the time they took the devices. I decided to remain silent.

I changed my sign-on station to Savile Row in London so I didn't have to go up north every week. A few weeks later I turned up at Savile Row as normal. It was very late as I'd been out for dinner with Charlotte. Sitting there, waiting for me, were two cops from Scotland, who had driven all the way down and had been there since 6 am. They'd had to wait at the station because they didn't know my London address. They almost missed me. They were so tired, sitting there reading books, they almost didn't spot me coming in.

'We need to talk to you, we need to serve you with this document.'

They were referring to the Regulation of Investigatory Powers (Scotland) Act and were once again ordering me to disclose my passwords. 'It's top secret,' they said, 'you can't tell anyone about this. You have to respond in two weeks.'

I spoke to my lawyers and then wrote to the police.

'Sorry, I have forgotten my passwords. I'd love to cooperate with you and if I remember them I'll let you know.'

That resulted in me being charged, under the RIPSA Act, for failing to disclose my passwords. I looked up the case history and the only people who had been charged with that before were terrorists and paedophiles. They dropped it eventually because they can't prove you haven't forgotten your passwords. I think most people might be sympathetic to the reality that if you haven't used your password for a year you might have forgotten it.

Police Scotland was a comedy turn. The more I heard about the investigation into me, the more I thought DI Robertson was like the Scottish equivalent of Inspector Clouseau. The police went to America at least twice, to see Duff and Phelps and Alastair Johnston. They went to South Africa to see Dave King – Jim and Jacqui went on all the trips. Robertson was loving this investigation, apparently. He was getting to meet all his Rangers heroes.

By September 2015 the police wanted to arrest us for a second time.

They went to Charlotte's mother's house to try to arrest me, but I wasn't there. They were going crazy, trying to phone Charlotte, as they didn't have my mobile number. 'Where's Craig?'

I was in London. They eventually got hold of Paul Kavanagh.

'They want to arrest you again,' he said. 'You have to come to Scotland.'

I got a flight up, met Paul and handed myself in. That spared me the company of Police Scotland travelling up to Glasgow with me. I met two female cops at a hotel car park in Paisley and they took me to Govan police station. I spent another night in a cell.

For the first time, the police tried to interview me. From 2011 I'd been willing to cooperate and had been cooperating where possible with the authorities and this was the first time the police tried to speak to me. They started asking all sorts of questions.

There is never, ever any benefit in speaking to the police. They have no interest in justice, no interest in the fact you might be innocent. They hope that you will say something that will help them convict you. That is their only interest.

I was determined not to say anything. They started asking me these questions and I think they were quite surprised I didn't even say 'no comment,' as they could have used that against me. I sat quietly through the whole interview. I think that disconcerted them somewhat.

It was so farcical it would have been funny, if the consequences hadn't been so serious.

I knew that, at the same time, Charles Green was being held in West Lothian. In stark contrast to my attitude, Charles had given them a seven-hour interview. It was so typical of Green. His legal advice must have been the same as mine. He just must have thought he could talk his way out of it.

When we arrived at court the following day it seemed at first like there were more police officers and photographers than angry punters. Once inside, I was asked if I wanted to be in a cell with Charles Green, under the sheriff court. I said no. The last thing I wanted was to be in a cell with him for a day.

Now there was a three-page charge sheet that was put before Glasgow Sheriff Court as we appeared in the dock.

As well as conspiracy, we were now charged with being involved in serious organised crime over the purchase of Rangers after Duff and Phelps took over as administrators in 2012.

David Whitehouse was also accused of conspiracy, while Green faced a separate fraud charge.

The prosecutors claimed that I conspired with Whitehouse and Green and others to acquire, 'through the administration of Rangers, control and ownership of the business and assets of Rangers for a consideration discounted from the true market value of said business and assets, all to the prejudice of the club's creditors.'

They accused Whitehouse of failing in his duty as an administrator of the club for acting in a manner that favoured the interests of Green and I.

Green also faced a further charge of fraud and one under the Companies Act.

Paul Clark was also charged with conspiracy and serious organised crime when he arrived in court the following day.

Once the hearing was over we asked if we could get away through the back door. The sheriff said it was fine by him, but would be up to the police. Predictably they said no. They love seeing themselves on telly and want the public spectacle, so when they go into the Masonic lodge they can say: 'I'm the guy that arrested Craig Whyte.'

I have no doubt about that.

At one stage, however, some fans, if that's what they were, got near the car and almost toppled it over. The car was shaking. The woman who was driving put her foot down quickly and got away.

It was difficult to see from my vantage point how many people were there. There were a lot of obscenities shouted but I suspect there were more police and media than fans.

A couple of weeks later indictments were served on us all, as well as David Grier, Gary Withey and Imran Ahmad. I think the police had tried to arrest Ahmad but he had already departed for Pakistan.

When I pored over the 50-page document I couldn't believe what I was reading. They were chucking everything at us, clearly in the hope that something would stick. It included things like serious organised crime, money laundering.

It was all utter garbage.

It emerged that Charles Green had got an agreement from the Rangers' board as part of his severance that they would cover his legal costs if he was ever accused of criminal offences. Rangers had to go to court to win in order to relieve them of the potential burden.

I applied for and was awarded legal aid, which some newspapers predictably tried to generate some fake outrage around. It was left to Paul Kavanagh to explain that the alleged charge was generally immaterial, as long as the applicants met the criteria.

Our next appearance was at the High Court in Edinburgh, where there were none of the chaotic scenes we'd witnessed at Glasgow Sheriff Court.

It was the first appearance when we were all together – and it was the first time I had seen any of them for years. On the way up to Edinburgh for the hearing I had met Paul Clark at Heathrow Airport, in the executive lounge. He came up to me, which I was quite surprised about. He was being very friendly. I met David Grier, too, on the way to court. I still disliked them intensely, but we were all in the same boat, and they were talking about information they had on the prosecutor Jim Keegan, and saying what a farce this was. We had a common enemy, so if there was a way to get out of the situation which meant cooperating with them, then fine.

Amid all of this – and a week on from my first appearance at the High Court – I was declared bankrupt.

It had taken two years to finalise. The High Court in London heard I had debts totalling £21 million. Ticketus were still able to recover around £2 million. It was a deeply wounding experience. There remains a stigma around bankruptcy and it was a situation in which I never imagined I would find myself. It prevented me from doing any business for a year. I just had to hope that it wouldn't affect my ability to resurrect my career when I eventually emerged out the other side.

Another long-running dispute was Rangers' case with HMRC. Two rulings on the EBT scheme had found in the club's favour but, as I had been warned in 2011, the tax office appealed and appealed until it won and that was the case in November 2014. At the Court of Session in Edinburgh, Lord Justice Ex-chairman Clerk, Lord Carloway, sitting with Lord Menzies and Lord Drummond Young, said that the now-outlawed scheme amounted to 'a mere redirection of earnings which did not remove the liability of employees to income tax'.

HMRC might have finally received the decision it wanted but at what cost – both to Rangers and the taxpayer? Could they really say that they had acted in the best interests of the public when they refused to have a discussion about repayment?

What the ruling also laid bare was that Rangers were heading for liquidation long before I came on the scene. Had David Murray remained in charge, the club was still heading for the rocks. The only question was how long it took to crash.

When it came to deciding how best to defend myself against the raft of charges against me, Paul Kavanagh's view was that Donald Findlay was the best. A former vice-chairman of Rangers, he was regularly among the top earners among the criminal Queen's Counsel each year. However, Kavanagh didn't hold out much hope of securing Findlay's services because of his football allegiances. Paul didn't ask him if he was open to being instructed.

Instead, he recommended Tony Graham, who was with us since 2014. Graham's *modus operandi* was to do a deal with the Crown, to get rid of it. I wasn't happy about that. I wasn't prepared to do any kind of deal under any circumstances.

The folly of that strategy in place of one that challenged the Crown's basis for the case became apparent on June 3, 2016 when we appeared in court in Glasgow. To my astonishment, charges were dropped against every one of my co-accused. I was going to be the only one prosecuted.

I sat alone in the dock as Bill McVicar, the advocate depute, confirmed there would be no further proceedings regarding Gary Withey and David Grier. (Whitehouse and Clark we also told charges had been dropped.) They immediately criticised the Crown for pursuing the charges, which they said were without foundation, and said that they would be looking to address the reputational damage caused.

McVicar said that Crown counsel were considering the position in relation to Green and added: 'I think it's fair to say any proceedings relating to Mr Green would be dealt with separately. Any proceedings against Mr Ahmad would be dealt with along with Mr Green.'

As I sat in the dock, the judge Lord Bannatyne appeared to lose patience with the prosecutor.

'Nobody seems to quite know what the current position is on anything,' he said. 'I want the Crown to make crystal clear what its position is. There seems to remain complete uncertainty. You are saying the only person left in the dock is Mr Whyte and I can proceed towards a trial?'

The situation with Withey was particularly galling for me. Withey got the case thrown out by Lord Bannatyne because the Crown had prior details of his defence as they had seized privileged correspondence between him and his lawyers in the civil case. The Crown argued against it being dropped and appealed against Lord Bannatyne's decision. They took it to the appeal court, where the judges agreed with Bannatyne's original ruling.

Unfortunately my lawyer hadn't made the same arguments. Withey only had the information because he was my lawyer. My counsel didn't see fit to make that argument. If he had, I might have seen the charges dropped against me early on. I wasn't terribly impressed, so we got rid of him there and then.

I retained the services of junior counsel Allan MacLeod.

Lord Bannatyne wanted a plea from me, but the Crown announced it intended to revise the charges. Without knowing the charges I faced, how was I supposed to enter a plea?

Allan MacLeod asked for an eight-week delay, but this was rejected. A new hearing was set for the end of July.

Outside there was the now-customary group of disgruntled people. One man shouted something about me being a 'dead man'.

Once again it seemed a special set of rules existed for me. I didn't want to see charges brought against anyone. It was ridiculous any of us had been subjected to such chastening treatment.

But as I contemplated what lay ahead, I thought back to the comments we'd heard that had been attributed to the Lord Advocate.

Could I really expect a fair trial in Glasgow, where in the eyes of some I had already been convicted before one word of evidence had been heard?

# EIGHTEEN

IT'S NOT WHAT happens to you, but how you react that matters.

The words of Epictetus, the Greek Stoic philosopher have chimed with me throughout my career, but as I steeled myself for the prospect of being the only person charged over the collapse of Rangers, I found myself falling back on those meditations.

Deal with what you can control. Accept calmly what life deals you. These were philosophies I related to. I had been reading such teachings since my late twenties. The great Stoic philosophers intrigued me. Epictetus had endured so much in his life. Born a slave, he wasn't imprisoned by the limitations of his status and studied philosophy. Once freed, he rose to eminence in Rome.

Roman emperor Marcus Aurelius's *Meditations* were another area of study. I've always had the philosophy that I wanted to improve myself a little bit all the time and I related to the theory that we're all flawed to an extent. I know I certainly am. I read a lot and aim to take on board something from everything I read. I also think about things deeply. I don't just accept the conventional point of view about anything without analysing it for myself. I think that's always served me well.

It certainly did during the months in the build up to the trial. I tried to envisage the worst that could happen – a guilty verdict and a prison sentence. I couldn't imagine being put in a cell would cause me great worry. As long as I had a pile of books to read, I didn't think of it as the end of the world. As long as I was kept safe I think I would have been fine.

I had a list of books I was going to read. I was going to work on my Spanish. I had a whole programme of things I was going to do.

I'd previously read Jeffrey Archer's accounts of his time in prison. He offered an interesting insight to life behind bars. One of my all-time favourite books is *The Count of Monte Cristo* by Alexandre Dumas. It is such a wonderful book. His account of wrongful imprisonment, escape from persecution and vengeance is quite something. It was a book I turned to during the period when it seemed the whole of Scotland was against me. Like Dumas' hero, I could have spent my time plotting revenge against those who had wronged me, but life is too short. Better instead to try to be positive in what you do next.

A lot of people were saying to me, 'How do you cope?'

The common view seemed to be that I should be depressed. Regardless of what people may have thought, I never was. I always kept a positive outlook. Nobody wants to go to prison, but there are worse things that can happen in your life. The fact that people had double-crossed me was now ancient history. I just wanted this whole business to be over with.

It had been six years since I started working on the takeover. I never wanted to think about it again.

All I could do was make sure that I had the best legal representation. After dispensing with Tony Graham, I needed a new QC.

Paul was using Donald Findlay on another case when the counsel asked him what was happening with the Rangers case?

Findlay said: 'I'm the only lawyer in Scotland who knows about football and the only one not involved.'

'Do you want to be involved?' Paul said.

'Yes,' he said.

It seemed a bit of a result, but we nearly got off on the wrong foot.

I first met Donald Findlay in Carlisle. My lawyer said: 'If we can convince Donald Findlay you are innocent, he will give his all for you. He is the hardest-working guy ever. We think you're innocent. If we can convince him, we'll be fine.'

I don't think we took to each other at all, initially. He would be too courteous to say this, but I suspect after I first met him he was thinking the same as every other Rangers fan. I don't think he liked me and I didn't fancy him much, either. He's quite a prickly character. It took a bit of time to get a rapport going. The first meeting was very formal and businesslike, but after two or three weeks, as Paul and Donald's junior, Alan had before him, Donald could see I hadn't profited at all from the Rangers situation. He was of the strong view that Murray and the previous board had messed up 'his club' as he referred to it. It didn't take too long to get him on board and we got on great after that. He is a really hard-working professional and I was very lucky to have him and the other members of the team on board. I was blessed with an amazing legal team.

Initially we tried to get the case thrown out altogether because the Crown did not allege that anyone had lost any money. We tried to argue that for there to be a fraud somebody had to lose, but the law in Scotland bizarrely dates back to a case history from 1925, to do with miners claiming an extra day's pay, which established that there doesn't have to be a loss for there to be a fraud. Lord Bannatyne said he couldn't throw it out because of that precedent. We went before three judges and argued again that you need to have a victim to have a crime, but they didn't agree. They said the 1925 judgment had served the law well. The example the Crown tried to use was that people are charged with mortgage fraud when they lie to the bank about their income and there's no loss in that situation, but there's still fraud. To my mind that shouldn't be a fraud either, but it is considered so in Scotland. That was the Crown's argument and the judges agreed with them.

Eighteen months after my first arrest the Crown still had not settled on the charges they planned to bring against me. At one hearing they announced they were revising the charges, but when we appeared in court in July 2016 they asked for another adjournment.

Lord Bannatyne tore into the prosecutor, Jim Keegan: 'This man is being asked to wait and see what the Crown are charging him with. I want to have a full explanation of how we have reached this position.'

Donald Findlay said: 'I can't advise my client until he knows what he is charged with.'

It seemed farcical – and caused me to wonder how the Crown secured any convictions if it carried on like this in every case.

The judge clearly thought they didn't know what they were doing.

With Donald Findlay on board I felt more confident about my chances, however hostile a jury might be.

A year on from the bankruptcy order, the restrictions were removed. I was still banned from being a company director in the UK, but that would not present an obstacle to future business dealings.

In the same month, at a hearing in the High Court in Glasgow, the Crown finally disclosed its revised charges. Alex Prentice QC was now heading the prosecution team. I was told Prentice was the Crown's top man. As I understood it, he liked to personally choose the cases he took on. However, in my case, in light of everything that had gone on, the Crown had dropped Keegan and the Lord Advocate had told Prentice to step in.

He confirmed as much when he told the court: 'The Lord Advocate asked that I step in ... that is what I will do.'

From the 50-page indictment they were left with two charges – one of fraud and a second allegation under the Companies Act.

The first accusation claimed I obtained a 'majority and controlling stake' in Rangers 'by fraud'. The charge dated from May 2010 to May 2011, listing various locations including Ibrox Stadium and Murray Park, as well as 'addresses meantime unknown' in Monaco and France. It said that my representatives and I pretended to then Rangers owner Sir David Murray and others that 'funds were available' to make all stipulated payments. It was claimed 'resources necessary' were available to meet a number of 'obligations' including £5 million for 'the playing squad'.

The second charge under the Companies Act centred on an £18 million payment in connection with the takeover.

The court heard the trial could last up to 12 weeks and was provisionally set for April the following year, in Glasgow.

When I analysed the charges, the first one didn't stack up because of the wording in the share purchase agreement. It had clearly stated third-party funds were being used. Murray's team hadn't cared where the money was coming from. If they had, they would have asked.

The second charge was the rarely-prosecuted offence of financial assistance, which only applied to public companies. The rationale behind this was that if you used the target company's assets to acquire that company, then any minority shareholders are losing out. For example, if an individual acquired 90 per cent of a company and used the assets of that business to pay the purchase price, then the remaining 10 per cent of the shareholders would be prejudiced. This didn't happen with Rangers as the purchase price was only a pound. There was also an advantage to the company in doing the deal, because it would rid the club of the Lloyds debt, as Ticketus replaced the bank on the balance sheet. How could they say the club was in a worse financial situation?

I didn't really understand the charge and my legal team struggled with it. We weren't convinced the Crown even understood it. If that was the case, then there was no way the jury were going to get their heads around it.

Another hearing was held in December, at the High Court in Edinburgh, where Allan MacLeod submitted a plea of not guilty to the two charges on my behalf. The case was scheduled to go to trial before judge Lady Stacey at the High Court in Glasgow in April 2017.

I still felt the whole thing was preposterous, but at least we had some clarity in terms of what I was up against.

Only after the charges were revised and a court date set was the Crown's evidence presented to my legal team. They were duty bound to disclose everything they had seized and there was a mountain of paperwork from dozens of different entities.

When it arrived there were 400,000 pages of documents to wade through. How do you even begin to go through that? It's a monumental task. I was lucky to have such a professional and hard-working legal team, but I wanted to give them and myself the best chance. I was giving them as much input as I could, wading through those documents and making sure my point of view got across. It was important that my team were buying into it and not going their own way. I was explaining things clearly to them and making sure they were able to represent me as best they could. As the Stoic philosophers said all those centuries earlier, I dealt with what I could, and the rest was not within my control, so why worry about it?

The Crown interviewed something like 300 prosecution witnesses. I saw all their interviews, all the witness statements, including the people from HMRC they had spoken to.

But, as I began to wade through the mountain of evidence, the truth began to emerge.

Finally I realised just what had been going on behind the scenes right before I got control of Rangers – what was really driving David Murray to finalise a deal.

And for the first time I discovered just why HMRC had been so keen to tip the club into administration.

It was all becoming clear. I was the fall guy right enough – but not in the way I had suspected.

# NINETEEN

THE POUND COIN spinning across the table. The pop of the champagne bottles.

I often thought back to the moment when Rangers became mine. It had all seemed too good to be true. And experience should have told me that when something seems too good to be true that's because it usually is.

At the time, however, I was thinking the deal had just got better. Yes, there were debts – far more than had first been claimed – but the deal was moving in my favour. In hindsight, it should have been a huge red flag that the Murray camp was so desperate to get rid of Rangers that they were giving it away for nothing. But I knew that it was going to be almost impossible to avoid administration. This way, I avoided paying a purchase price that would end up as money wasted.

Reading through the trial documents, I suddenly saw what had really been going on.

The bank was effectively liquidating Murray International Holdings. David Murray was basically working for Bank of Scotland to liquidate his company. It wasn't a formal liquidation, but he was winding it up. He was trying to get any assets he could out of the bank-controlled company into another of his own – Murray Capital, I believe. The bank told him that if he wanted to get Murray Metals into Murray Capital, his 100 per cent-owned company, he could buy it back for a pound, providing he sold Rangers by April 30, 2011.

Murray was on a deadline to close the deal. That was why they were putting us under so much pressure. The bank wanted out of Rangers so desperately and they had given him that incentive.

I knew nothing about that.

All the evidence was contained on a hard disc and my legal team and I were going through it all. Some items they flagged up to me, while I would highlight the importance of others to them. I was seeing things and just thinking, 'wow.' I couldn't believe what had been going on behind the scenes.

I was suddenly getting access to documents and emails that the other side never thought would come to light. It was quite shocking.

While I thought I had agreed a capped fee of £500,000 for the administration of Rangers, it is now clear that HMRC were willing to remove the cap to the same people for that administration. At the very least it would seem to me that this placed advisers I thought were mine in a conflicted position. Duff and Phelps estimated a fee of £3 million for administration in their paperwork. It is fair to say (and this I either did not fully comprehend or was not made clear to me) that HMRC would in no circumstances accept a controlled administration and were out to make an example of the club.

It is for others to comment on the position that Duff and Phelps were in and the outcome that resulted. However that may be the result of the situation was their receipt of a fee some £2.5 million higher than the capped fee which had been my agreed position with them.

My personal feelings regarding what happened, whatever the rights and wrongs objectively, were a strong sense of breach of trust and betrayal of our professional relationship. Given that the consequences certainly cost me ownership of the club and may well have been an issue in its liquidation, the strength of my feelings is I hope understandable.

They were getting paid by Rangers every month. They probably got £500,000 worth of fees out of Rangers before administration. There should have been no question of loyalties.

If I had stayed in control and it had been a quick administration, Duff and Phelps only stood to get a £500,000 fee. They ended up getting multiple times that, once you factored in the legal costs.

It was and remains my belief that Rangers could have been saved. Whether the issue of the scale of fees offered or paid by either party was a factor in decisions taken or advice given remains moot and not something I would wish to comment further on. Nor indeed could I speculate as to the stage my advisers were aware of the potential differences in renumeration available from the different options.

They were happy to agree to cap the fees initially, knowing that once the club entered administration that agreement would no longer stand.

I was completely in the dark. I didn't even know MCR were selling up to Duff and Phelps. They only told me after it had gone through and they changed their name, in the autumn of 2011.

Right up until HMRC put the club into administration, I supported Duff and Phelps' appointment. I thought it was the best outcome for the club – and for me. Yet, within 48 hours of entering administration, employees of Rangers were told not to talk to me. People were calling me and saying, 'Duff and Phelps have told me not to talk to you anymore'. I realised then

I was cut out of it completely.

When I met David Grier afterwards he put all the blame onto HMRC. I've got a witness statement from Grier in which he supports his position. I had to take what he was saying at face value.

By the time we all ended up in court we had actually been speaking to each other again, because we had a common enemy in the Crown.

It was only later, when I saw the police statements from HMRC, that I saw a different version of events. What David Grier had told them seemed to me to contrast completely with what he had been saying to me.

With their public pronouncements and their evidence to a high court judge, Duff and Phelps had made life very difficult for me. Take the Ticketus deal. They tried to say they knew nothing about it, and then were forced to try to claim they thought Ticketus were only being used to raise working capital. There were reams of evidence to the contrary.

Only the Crown will know why it decided not to proceed with the action against the administrators. Having seen how they operate, I have my suspicions.

They needed a fall guy, and I was already the pantomime villain in the media. Why confuse matters by trying to establish a wider conspiracy? Keep it simple. Present the bad guy to a jury in Glasgow and watch them exact revenge of the death of the establishment club.

When I sifted through the evidence before me, I experienced a rush of emotions – anger, annoyance, a feeling of betrayal, bitterness.

There was a flipside, though. This evidence we had been presented with – the Crown's own case against me – would now form the basis for the defence. We started building evidence to support my case.

My trial would be unlike anything Scottish football had seen before. The latest episode in the Rangers saga would be compelling viewing. Who would take the stand? Who knew what? Who would tell the truth?

# TWENTY

COURT FOUR, HIGH COURT, Glasgow, 20 April 2017

When the time came to face the 15 people in whose hands my fate lay, I was calm.

I had made the decision to try to have as normal a time in Glasgow as anyone could when his liberty and reputation is at risk. I stayed at the Radisson Hotel, in the city centre, close to the River Clyde. I was determined not to be prisoner to my circumstances and remain locked inside my room for the duration. I resolved to go for morning runs along the river to Glasgow Green and every day I would walk to court.

Once I arrived at the High Court, near the Saltmarket, it helped that the staff were polite and courteous. I was given my own little room with a sofa. That helped me compose myself and adjust to the situation. The courtroom was packed with media and members of the public. I'm sure the Rangers fans among them were keen to find out what happened to their club. There was no heckling or abuse. It was civil.

The jury consisted of eight men and seven women. I tried to scrutinise their faces, to work out whether they had any preconceptions about me. Trial judge Lady Stacey asked them several questions to determine whether there was any conflict of interest.

'There has been some degree of publicity about Mr Whyte and Rangers – putting it at its broadest – over the last number of years,' she said.

'Do you know Mr Whyte? Do you know anyone personally who may be a witness? During May 2010 and May 2011, were you a shareholder, bond holder or season ticket holder of Rangers? Ask yourself: is there any good reason why you cannot be an impartial member of this jury.'

She also told the jurors to 'put out of mind' anything they may have read or heard previously about the case.

Once they were sworn in we were ready to begin. The trial would start the following day.

The first witness was Walter Smith. I suspected the tactic was to play on the emotions of the jurors. It was the only reason I could think why the Crown would call him. He didn't know anything about what went on. He wasn't there during my time in charge. I also think the Crown was going for maximum coverage. Somehow the publicity seems to seduce people and I wondered if the prosecutors wanted to make as big a circus out of the case as possible.

Walter Smith spoke of the meeting we had before the takeover. Perhaps the inference was that I was more interested in the financial state of the club than the playing side.

He was helpful because he told the court the club was in a bad way when I bought it. He spoke of Rangers' dire financial state when he went back to the club as manager in 2007. The overdraft was at £30 million and even though he brought eight trophies to Rangers and got them to a European final, the overdraft still stood at around £18 million when he left.

During breaks in proceedings I was able to retreat to my little room. It meant I didn't have to mingle with the media.

When it was Donald Findlay's turn to speak to Smith, he asked him whether he remembered how Rangers had done in their bid to qualify for the Champions League after his departure. Smith said: 'I know they lost one of the games, but I couldn't tell you accurately, I was on holiday at the time.'

'Do you even remember whether Rangers ended up in the Europa League?' Findlay asked.

Smith said: 'I don't think they ended up in the Europa League.'

'That would have been a major disappointment, not just in footballing terms, but in financial terms,' Findlay said.

'Yes, it is a major disappointment to any club, they are trying to qualify for the Champions League. That's a massive thing, not just financially but for the club overall, for the club's stature, and then next the Europa League, so it's a big blow to everyone if you have no European football,' Smith said.

Smith said that in his first stint as manager David Murray had been 'very hands-on'. Second time around it was Martin Bain who was dealing with the running of the club in his position as chief executive.

When they came to discuss Rangers being up for sale, Findlay said: 'There wasn't exactly a stampede of people coming through the door wanting to buy Rangers Football Club, was there, Mr Smith?'

'No.'

Findlay said there were no foreign billionaires wanting to buy Rangers. He put it to Smith that there were no other bidders.

'No.'

Raising the issue of the £30 million overdraft in 2007, Findlay said: 'That was, on any view, a major financial burden hanging round the club. More football clubs are in debt, rather than profit. Why is that?'

Smith said he supposed the banks allowed it to happen, and that, speaking for Rangers, 'football clubs are prepared to handle that level of debt'.

When Smith was asked what he would have done if two £7.5 million players were injured early in the season and out for the rest of the season, he said: 'Panic. There are no guarantees.'

Findlay said buying expensive players with no guarantee of European success could result in disaster. Smith agreed.

'So throwing money at it is a stupid idea,' Findlay said.

'It is a gamble,' Smith said.

'A football club has to operate at a level that is realistic, that would be a sound approach,' Findlay said.

My counsel asked the former manager whether he knew the bank no longer wished to bankroll Rangers. Smith said he'd known two to three years earlier. 'Donald Muir had joined the club. He was there to implement certain cuts to make the club more viable,' he said.

Findlay produced minutes of board meetings from November 2010 and March 2011, which laid bare Rangers' financial situation. Transcripts from the March meeting showed Rangers faced a wages cap over an £18 million bank overdraft, which was stopping them from extending the contracts of key players. The club was able to spend only £300,000 on youth development, when it was estimated Celtic were spending £2 million. The bank was asking for a £14.6 million salary restriction, yet Martin Bain was warning that £18 million was needed to rebuild the squad.

At one point, ex-chairman John McClelland said new investment was going to be needed just to keep the club 'afloat'. Findlay put it to Smith that this happened months before I took over the club.

He said: 'Where is anybody going to get £18 million from?'

Findlay got Smith to agree that trying to find £18 million

when you're already £18 million in debt would be driving debt to the level it was beforehand.

Smith also agreed with Findlay that the club's finances were in a 'perilous state'. Smith said the club had been trying to handle this issue, but the challenge they faced was trying to compete while controlling spending.

Donald Findlay told the court about Ally McCoist's contract and how if he did not take over from Smith as manager it would cost the club an 'enormous' amount of money. Smith was shown the sums involved, but they were not disclosed to the wider court.

'Somebody has put the club in a position that if they don't follow the line of succession it is going to cost the club a small fortune.'

Smith said: 'I had no idea that was the case.'

'Extraordinary isn't it?' Findlay said.

'Mr McCoist obviously negotiates his own contracts, so he's possibly a bit brighter than I am,' Smith replied.

Next up was McCoist.

He spoke of his frustration at not getting the players he wanted and said we bid too low for the ones he'd targeted – the type of woes I'm sure you hear at any football club over the course of a season.

The Crown's claim in the indictment was that I didn't buy any players. McCoist acknowledged that of course we bought players, we bought lots of players. I'm convinced a lot of Rangers fans forget that. We signed and resigned lots of players. We had a decent team.

Findlay showed him a document proving the player budget had gone up – after I took over – from £15.4 million to £21 million.

Findlay said: 'To suggest that money was not spent on the squad does not seem to be supported by these figures.'

McCoist said: 'I did not say that money was not spent on the squad.'

Findlay replied: 'No, no, you may not, but other people are trying to.'

When they moved on to discuss McCoist's contract, he admitted he had no conversations about the terms of that deal with me, even though I was the owner.

McCoist said the managerial contract was put in front of him and he was asked to sign it by Martin Bain. Findlay put it to McCoist that it was unusual that the former owner's chief executive was asking him to sign a contract. Findlay said: 'Does that not strike you as a bit odd?'

McCoist replied: 'Well, when you put it like that it might not seem the norm.'

Donald McIntyre took the stand and admitted to the court that the bank wanted out of Rangers. The former finance director at first tried to wriggle around the issue, but said: 'They were threatening to withdraw the bank facilities if the independent board committee did not sanction the transaction with Craig Whyte.'

Findlay challenged him: 'If that's not the bank wanting out, what is it?'

Eventually, when asked if Lloyds were 'putting the squeeze on the company', McIntyre replied: 'Correct.'

He also told the court that Rangers had used Ticketus previously as a revenue stream, with up to £5 million being advanced by the company against season tickets at any one time. He said he thought the costs of this credit line to be about £160,000.

Findlay put it to the witness that the club's arrangement with Ticketus was 'kept hush-hush from the fans'.

'There was no need to disclose it,' McIntyre said.

McIntyre also confirmed he was aware of huge Murray

Group debts in 2009. He agreed the Murray Group debt was hundreds of millions of pounds, and that their main lenders were Lloyds.

McIntyre also disclosed that, at a time when Rangers' debts were about £27 million, bonuses had been paid out after the UEFA Cup final in 2008.

Referring to McCoist's lucrative deal, Findlay asked McIntyre if it was 'fiscal prudence' to pay a sum of money for someone not getting a job. McIntyre said: 'No.'

McIntyre said he was aware of the potential tax liability as far back as October 2010 and admitted that the possibility of administration had been discussed as far back as that time.

Following McIntyre was David Murray. I expected Murray to be hostile. His legacy was on the line here. When discussing the ruinous EBT tax scheme, Murray admitted that it allowed the club to sign players it couldn't otherwise afford. Asked about the scheme's purpose, he said: 'I would not say to reduce tax. It gave us an opportunity to get players that we perhaps would not be able to afford.'

That seemed to challenge the view of Lord Nimmo Smith, who chaired the SPL commission on the EBT scheme, which examined whether the club had broken rules by failing to disclose them. While it was found that all clubs were required to declare contracts to promote sporting integrity, Nimmo Smith said Rangers had not gained any unfair competitive advantage from operating side-letter arrangements and nor were any players ineligible to play in matches. Rangers were fined £250,000, but the club was not stripped of any titles. Dave King had previously also dismissed the claim that Murray was now making.

Murray clearly had a line he had to stick to. He had been on TV saying he had been duped. He tried to carry that on in court. Apparently the Crown didn't speak to all the witnesses beforehand, they just relied on the police statements. It was showing in the Crown witnesses' evidence.

When Alex Prentice concluded his examination of David Murray you could have sold tickets for what was coming next. David Murray and Donald Findlay had their own history. Now my QC, the former vice-chairman of Rangers, had the opportunity to take his old boss to task over who was to blame for the demise of his beloved club. It promised to be compelling viewing.

# TWENTY-ONE

THE APPEARANCE OF Murray had clearly captured everyone's attention. The press and public galleries were packed. When the time came for Donald Findlay to begin his cross-examination you could sense the anticipation.

Findlay honed in on why Murray had not sought to challenge me on the Ticketus aspect of the deal once he found out. The QC described our contact as 'cordial' – even after Murray claimed he became aware of the funding arrangement. Their exchanges grew increasingly terse as Murray tried to reject Findlay's assessment of why he hadn't raised the subject. Findlay asked Murray repeatedly why he had failed to raise his concerns about the Ticketus deal with me when we met over lunch late in 2011.

Murray at first tried to claim he did not become aware of the Ticketus deal until a year after he had sold the club. But he later agreed it could have been in October 2011.

'I'm just wondering if you could explain to the jury any reason why you would not have raised it with him at the time of the lunch,' Findlay said.

Murray claimed he had set out his issues with Ticketus in a letter to me, which he wasn't able to produce.

Findlay said: 'No, I'm concerned with sitting down, across

a table, having lunch in Monaco. Why wouldn't you have discussed it with him face to face?'

Murray said: 'I can't see any reason why I wouldn't have done, had I been aware.'

Findlay asked Murray if our relationship soured after he discovered the Ticketus deal. Murray tried to say we had no relationship.

'None at all? In any form?' Findlay said.

'I don't recall that,' said Murray.

Findlay showed Murray a series of text messages between us dated from October 2011. Over 10 pages of text messages, we discussed the Rangers tax case, the Bain case, we mentioned phoning each other, and exchanged Christmas greetings.

'Looking at the series of messages, would it seem possible that there was at least contact between you and Mr Whyte on the November 4, that you wanted to discuss the tax case?' Findlay said.

In one message on November 13, Murray had said to me: 'Let's ensure that we remain tight on the HMRC situation, don't want any media or internet speculated comment for it could totally undermine any chance of a possible negotiation.'

'So at the very least of it, there appears to have been contact between you and Mr Whyte,' Findlay said. 'Why did you not mention Ticketus?'

Murray tried to avoid answering the question. Findlay had to say to him: 'I'm sorry, you're in the witness box and these are the rules.'

Findlay kept probing why, even when we had met for lunch, Ticketus had not been discussed. Murray tried to claim that he'd brought up the issue of funds then, but it was about 'funds not going into the club'.

'I asked where the working capital had gone, that was where the major part of the conversation took place,' Murray said.

After more blustering from Murray, Findlay said: 'Simple question: After you had discovered about the Ticketus deal, there is contact of a reasonably cordial nature between you and Mr Whyte. Clearly, having discovered about the Ticketus deal, which struck at the very heart of what you wanted for the club, we might have thought your relationship with Mr Whyte would have been less than cordial.'

Murray again mentioned the letter he'd apparently sent and apologised for changing the subject. Findlay said: 'Changing the subject in these courts is what we call not answering the question.'

Findlay also challenged Murray's earlier claim in court that he was aware of no 'third party' being involved in the deal. He showed Murray the share purchase agreement. Findlay said that there were several versions of the document, the earliest of which made provision for Murray to be honorary life president of Rangers. It mentioned cash coming from me and a 'third party'.

'Have you read this? Findlay asked.

'Not for some time,' Murray said. 'I will have read it at some time, yes.'

Mike McGill had signed the share purchase agreement. Findlay said: 'Interestingly, you didn't sign it, did you? You know what was in it?'

'Yes,' Murray said.

Findlay said: 'Your advisers knew perfectly well that the money was coming from Mr Whyte and somebody else.'

'That's not what they told me,' Murray said.

Findlay said: 'So your advisers sign an agreement that says the money is coming from his own resources and third party resources. Is that Mr Whyte's resources?'

Murray said: 'You could read that in many ways.'

Findlay also produced an email sent by 'David Fraser' – an

email address used by Murray – which appeared to show him putting pressure on the Rangers independent committee to sell, saying that I was threatening to withdraw.

The email said: 'Need to get this over the line or the purchaser will walk away. Nothing is perfect but we do not have a viable alternative. The fallout is extremely serious.'

Murray agreed that some of the independent committee were trying to block the deal. He agreed that he 'more than likely' had described my offer as 'the only game in town'.

The packed court was silent throughout these exchanges – it was compelling theatre.

Murray's evidence went into a second day. As I walked to court the following morning, a man approached me in a threatening manner. He was being a bit creepy, telling me where I'd gone for dinner the previous night, as if he'd been following me. I notified police, who detained him. It was an isolated incident. For the most part, I was able to walk about unmolested. Inside court, I was in the dock waiting for proceedings to begin when Lady Stacey informed the court that a juror had fallen ill and we'd adjourn for the day.

When court resumed the next day, Donald Findlay honed in on Murray's previous evidence, when he had claimed he didn't know the money came from Ticketus and he 'categorically' would not have sold to me had he known.

Findlay produced a note handwritten by a lawyer and someone he told the court was one of Murray's 'closest advisors'. It was the note from David Horne, saying: 'Octopus discussion w/CW re £15m possible facility.'

Murray said he had never seen the note.

Findlay told him: 'Octopus was Ticketus. So it would seem that one of your closest advisers, David Horne, was aware Mr Whyte may be looking for a partner, a possibility of £15 million by somebody called Octopus.'

Murray said: 'It appears by that note. I've never seen or heard of that.'

'Does that not seem a bit surprising?' Findlay said.

Murray said he couldn't say.

Horne had also appeared to suggest in a note that if Rangers lost a legal battle with the tax authorities, the club might have to consider administration, and that Murray would be the 'PR front man'. Findlay put it to Murray: 'Here is one of your closest advisers contemplating administration if the tax case goes against Rangers, and contemplating you being the PR front man, and nobody bothered to tell you. He didn't tell you that Ticketus could be involved in the deal and he didn't tell you that you might have to front up the PR in case of administration. Here is Mr Horne knowing about Ticketus in 2010 and you don't know until 2012.'

Murray, becoming visibly irritated, said: 'Not from a scribbled note.'

Findlay also drew attention to evidence that Martin Bain had his notice period increased from 12 to 39 months by the Rangers board after Murray stepped down from the day-to-day running of the club.

And he raised a letter Dave King sent to the independent committee a fortnight before the takeover. King said he was concerned 'about the source of funds' for the wider deal. King raised the prospect of a police investigation.

Findlay asked Murray: 'Were you aware of any talk about a police investigation?'

He replied: 'Not at all.'

Murray said he was aware of a meeting in London when it was expected that King would make an offer, but it 'never materialised'. He added: 'He had every opportunity to match, equal or buy shares in the club prior to Mr Whyte.'

Findlay also put to Murray evidence that Alastair Johnston

had described the playing squad as a 'shambles' and warned that I had not been given the opportunity to understand the issues facing the club.

My counsel read from an email from Johnston to Murray in March 2011 in which he said: 'There has been in my opinion no credible opportunity for Craig Whyte in this process that would have allowed him to totally understand the issues that he will face as majority owner of Rangers Football Club.' These included the 'shambles' of a playing squad, the upkeep of Ibrox stadium and health-and-safety-related maintenance.

Putting these correspondences into context, Findlay said to Murray: 'In general terms, you entrusted the club to a board that you believed were capable of following the plan that you had left in place, but they bring in no investment, their playing squad ends up as a shambles and this is two months before the deal with Mr Whyte, and the chairman has handed a huge extension to the chief executive. You were being let down by people who didn't have a clue what they were doing when running Rangers.'

As he wound up his cross-examination, Findlay berated the actions of the former board. He put it to Murray: 'From you stepping down as chairman and Craig Whyte taking over, what had these men done to your football club, Sir David. What had they done to our club?'

It was powerful stuff – coming from one Rangers man to another.

Murray could only reply that he thought the football side was reasonable and another alternative plan to raising cash would have been sought.

It was a strange performance from Murray. He was economical with the truth about certain things to say the least, but Donald Findlay made mincemeat of him. And he could have been even harder on him.

However, as I watched Murray struggling out of court on his crutches, I almost felt a little sorry for him. He looked like an old man, his Rangers legacy in tatters. Perhaps Findlay got the balance right – had he been more harsh, people may have felt sympathy toward him, given his situation.

It was tough at times to sit there though, listening to him. He had claimed there was no incentive to get the steel business back by selling Rangers. It would be interesting to see if any subsequent witnesses contradicted that statement.

# TWENTY-TWO

IT DIDN'T TAKE long for Murray's evidence to come under question. Ian Shanks, Rangers' former 'relationship manager' for Lloyds bank, confirmed a deal had been in place for Murray to buy back his metals business since April 2010.

The court heard how Murray's crumbling empire was being restructured under the name 'Project Charlotte'. The jury listened as they were told that Sir David wanted Murray Metals spun out of his Murray International Holdings group so he could take back control. It was then disclosed, as I had found out in the weeks before the trial, that the bank would only consider the move if it got its money back from Rangers.

'That was always in agreement as part of Project Charlotte,' Shanks said.

Findlay put it to him: 'There was an agreement whereby Sir David Murray could get his own metals business back for £1 … providing Rangers was sold or for some other reason the bank debt was eliminated.'

'Correct,' Shanks said.

It was in January 2011 that Sir David wrote to Lloyds to ask them to 'spin out' Murray Metals, even though there hadn't been a sale. However, this was rejected by the bank.

Findlay said: 'It seems clear that the only way to be sure of getting the metal business for £1 is to do the Rangers deal. That's an incentive to get the deal done, is it not?'

'I would agree, yes,' Shanks said.

A letter from Alastair Johnston was disclosed, in which the former chairman had referred to the Rangers board as bank 'stooges', running the club into the ground in the months before the takeover. Johnston drafted the note, intended for Shanks, in January 2011. In it, he said the bank wanted to 'drain every penny' from the club and 'throttle it into submission'.

The letter, sent to Rangers board members, said: 'We are all masquerading as directors of Rangers Football Club, acting in collaboration to form a board, while in reality we have been acting as stooges in facilitating the bank's sole objective to drain every single penny out of the club until the debt has been paid down, or once Rangers as a thriving entity has been throttled into submission.'

Johnston also claimed Lloyds had taken over Murray's 85 per cent shareholding in the club. Asked about the letter, Shanks said he couldn't remember whether it had ever been sent to him, but admitted he recognised 'the sentiments'. But he said: 'The bank was not taking every penny, as Alastair comments. I think the club was operating under difficult financial circumstances, but it was still operating.'

The jury heard how Murray Group had to place people on the board of Rangers to help manage the club while the bank set limits for borrowing and wage bills. An email from Shanks' predecessor, David McEwan, showed how frustrated Lloyds had been with the way the club was run.

The email, from October 2009, said: 'There is a continuing expectation and belief that the club can operate beyond its means with impunity.'

There were more revelations when Shanks came back for

a second day's testimony. It emerged Rangers had hid the use of Ticketus funds to buy Nikica Jelavić from Rapid Vienna in 2010. In correspondence between Shanks and Martin Bain there was mention of the transfer and how the Austrian club 'required the balance of transfer funds' to be 'cashbacked'.

I sat there wondering why the Crown was calling such witnesses. By the second week of the trial they should have been getting into the nitty-gritty of the charge, but all that had been revealed was what a mess Rangers had been long before I got there.

When Mike McGill took the stand I wondered where his loyalties would lie. I could understand Murray's stance – he had a position to defend. How far would McGill go?

The answer was far further than I imagined.

He defended the Murray position to the hilt, claiming I said to him personally that I would fund the deal out of my own money. He insisted there was no 'fire sale'. And he stated that he was 'appalled' when he learned about Ticketus.

This was hard to take. I barely spoke to Mike McGill before the takeover.

However, I was fortunate that I had Donald Findlay on my side. He ripped McGill to shreds. He asked where the evidence for these statements was. Did I send him any emails?

During his cross-examination, Findlay teased out all sorts of information. McGill acknowledged that when Bain's contract had been extended without running it past shareholders, company law had been broken.

Asked by Findlay if it was a straightforward example of fiscal imprudence, McGill said: 'Yes, it would breach the Companies Act.'

Findlay also referred to a confidential email dated December 2010, from Johnston to McGill and other board members, which talked about a £64 million investment, including a player acquisition fund of £25 million and working capital of £11.8 million.

'It's fantasy, isn't it?' Findlay said.

'Without anyone to fund it, yes,' said McGill.

The 'non-embarrassment' clause that Murray's team had insisted was included in the share purchase agreement so that I would not be publicly critical of Murray's time at the club was revealed to the jury. McGill accepted this was 'unusual'.

Perhaps most damaging to the Crown's case was McGill's admission that Murray or Rangers carried out no financial background checks on me before the deal was done.

'We were able to do very limited due diligence on Mr Whyte,' he said, confirming my suspicions that they had left it to journalists to do the digging.

McGill added: 'But we found nothing to suggest or indicate to us that Mr Whyte did not have the funds.'

In another email submitted in evidence it was said that if the deal went through and I did not fulfil a pledge to put in £10 million – which the bank was aware I had not guaranteed – then I, and not Murray or the bank, would take the wrath of the fans.

They certainly delivered on that front.

Findlay probed McGill on the bonuses some of the Rangers board received for getting the club off Murray's books. Bain received £360,000, while Horne got £160,000. McGill and Donald Muir received bonuses too, but McGill said those were not solely for the sale of the club.

The court also heard how McGill responded to an email sent by Horne on April 21, 2011.

My QC also zeroed in on what McGill knew about other investors. The jury heard about an email that dealt with technicalities of the deal, with my team seeking a concession over an asset. Horne had asked McGill whether the Murray Group should agree to the concession.

McGill replied: 'Given that the useless twits don't have the funds, it appears academic – why not?'

That seemed to suggest he knew I didn't have my own bottomless pit of cash. In another email sent to Horne, Murray Group's legal advisers Dundas Wilson, and others a month before the sale, McGill said of my bid: 'In simple terms we have no idea if they have the funds to run the club after purchase.'

The jury heard of documents, which showed that the Murray Group knew we might use £15 million of borrowed cash to fund the deal.

McGill was shown a handwritten note from Alastair Johnston, which was sent to other members of the board in the weeks before the sale. The note appeared to confirm that Octopus was providing £15 million.

It was very similar to the note written by Horne.

McGill tried to dismiss the significance of the notes as referring to 'working capital'.

The court was also told that McGill had emailed Horne and other Murray officials, including chairman Sir David Murray, on April 6, 2011 about discussions he had with David Grier concerning the 'big tax case'. The email said: 'DG [Grier] let it slip that this opinion was required for Craig Whyte's other investors.'

Findlay said to him: 'So as of April 6, 2011, you knew Mr Whyte had other investors?'

McGill said: 'That is certainly what the note says, yes.'

When asked if anyone at Rangers or the Murray Group had asked who those investors were, McGill said: 'I do not remember that, no. I cannot recall why I didn't do anything.'

Findlay went on: 'Mr Johnston seemed to know about Octopus and the funding of £15 million, and Mr Horne knew about the funding. Everybody knew – you, Sir David and others – that Mr Whyte had investors.'

He asked if anyone had asked me about the £15 million ahead of the sale.

McGill said: 'I don't believe we ever sought that clarity.'

Asked if anyone had checked with Octopus to say, 'What's this all about?' McGill said: 'We did not.' Pressed by Findlay that this would have been the obvious thing to do, McGill said: 'With the benefit of hindsight, yes.'

In another email sent on February 16, 2011, to Donald Muir and others, McGill spoke of his frustration that certain members of the board – notably Alastair Johnston – did not want the deal to proceed.

Findlay even managed to get McGill to admit that it was 'possible' Murray's team might sack the old board to force the sale through, if the independent board committee were being downright obstructive.

When my former lawyer Gary Withey gave evidence, he backed my position that the Murray team were desperate to close the deal.

Withey said: 'This was the only deal I had been in where the vendor was pushing more than the purchaser. Mr Whyte was not pushing, he did not seem to care. I have never been pushed so hard on any deal. They were desperate to get the deal over the line.'

He added: 'They did not ask how they were financing the deal. They didn't seem to care.'

Describing his frustrations at not being able to thoroughly examine the club before the deal went through, Withey said: 'I didn't trust MIH [Murray group]. We couldn't get under the bonnet. Then there was [the question of] what if the club goes bust? I had never seen that before.'

Withey told the court what he'd told me right at the outset: that he thought I was 'mad' to get involved with a football club.

Next up was Ross Bryan, of Octopus, who had been instrumental in getting the Ticketus involvement. He clearly did not want to be there. Under cross-examination he said it would have been better if Ticketus had been kept confidential.

Phil Betts, when he took the stand, agreed.

'They wanted, for commercial reasons [for it] to be kept private, and you were aware of that?' Findlay asked Betts.

'Yes,' Betts said.

'It wasn't because anyone was trying to hide anything illegal, it was because they didn't want the public at large – football fans – to know that they were giving 10 per cent of their money to an English fund, and you knew that,' said Findlay.

Betts agreed and also confirmed that the non-disclosure agreement was not unusual in the world of business, and that I was obligated to keep quiet.

'And, of course, by keeping it quiet he misled the other side of the deal?' asked Findlay.

'Yes,' Betts said.

'But was the bank paid?' Findlay asked.

'Yes,' Betts said.

'And was the club in a better position than it had been before the deal?'

'Yes,' Betts said. He went on to say how our business plan involved getting rid of the club's debt, making it more attractive to investors, saving on paying the bank interest and hoping to have a run in the Champions League to bring in revenue.

'The bank is paid, the stadium is fixed, the tax case was appealed, players were signed – and Rangers should never have gone near Malmo,' said Findlay, jokingly referencing our Swedish disaster in the Champions League qualifiers.

A cornerstone of the Crown's case was that I had left the club in a worse state. Yet its own witnesses were testifying that this simply wasn't the case.

David Horne, Murray's lawyer and the one whose handwritten note had cast doubt on claims they had not known of Ticketus's involvement, told the court he had known for months I was dealing with the firm, but he claimed he believed the £15 million was for working capital. And he admitted to Findlay that nothing had been spent on due diligence by the Murray side.

After 17 Crown witnesses, Advocate Depute Alex Prentice announced he had concluded the prosecution case. Originally the Crown had intended to call hundreds of witnesses for a trial expected to last 12 weeks. As the trial progressed, however, they informed our side that they were scaling it back – I think because they realised how badly it was going.

The original case they set out to make was that Rangers was a good, solid business and they were talking about the club's 'gearing' not being very high – as if a Glasgow jury was going to understand that financial technicality. Gearing is the percentage of debts versus assets. Rangers, on paper at least, looked like it had a lot of assets. The stadium was valued at £100 million and the training ground £20 million, giving a net position of something like £70 million. But in reality, how much could you sell Ibrox Stadium for? It's not worth anything to anyone other than Rangers FC. It's a listed building, it's not in one of the best areas of Glasgow. What else would anyone do with it? Duff and Phelps sold the stadium for £1.5million. It wasn't worth £100 million, only one and a half percent of that. So the Crown's argument that the gearing was only 20 per cent just wasn't valid. It was coming from prosecutors who were not businessmen. They did not understand the nuances of such things and, in any event, that argument was just washed away when Donald McIntyre came in.

As soon as Donald Findlay started questioning McIntyre the extent of the financial peril the club was in prior to my arrival became clear. The old board were considering administration, they had no money, the bank wanted to pull the plug. It was fucked, basically.

McIntyre's testimony was fundamentally damaging to the Crown's claim that the club had been in a sound financial state before the takeover. After his testimony, they cut back the number of witnesses dramatically. With that, the Crown's original argument fell away completely. Now, after just over a month, it was done. I felt, apart from David Murray and Mike McGill, whose evidence had been called into question by the statements of others, no one said anything negative against me. One of the security guards asked me at one point whether some of the Crown witnesses had been there for the defence, such was the nature of the evidence.

The Crown case was so weak we naturally put in a 'no case to answer' submission, once the jury had left the court. A defendant can seek to be acquitted without having to submit a defence if there is a feeling the prosecution has not proved its case. It was rejected by Lady Stacey. We didn't really expect anything more. Judges don't want to do anything controversial that might give grounds for appeal. They have their professional pride and the last thing they want to do is make a decision that is later reversed on appeal.

It was down to me now. A chance to prove my innocence. Or did I even have to?

# TWENTY-THREE

WHILE MOST OF the country was enjoying the spring bank holiday, my legal team and I were holed up in Paul Kavanagh's office in St Enoch Square, Glasgow. It was the night before we expected the Crown to conclude its case. The debate was over whether I should give evidence or not.

It was going to be my decision, but we went around the table so everyone could give their opinion. With me were Donald Findlay, Allan MacLeod and Victoria Young, his two juniors, and Paul. If I didn't give evidence and the verdict went against me, I would regret it forever. On the other hand, the Crown case had been so weak we were in a very strong position. What if I took the stand and made a mess of it?

We conducted a mock examination, with Findlay asking me questions as if I was giving evidence. At least one of the counsel thought I should give evidence, but the over-riding view from Paul and Donald was that I should not. That was the decision I came to.

Going to court every day for several weeks is a strange experience. Even though your liberty and your reputation is at stake, it's impossible not to form some rapport with the people who form part of your day-to-day existence.

Once I left my small room in the court, I always had two G4S security people standing either side of me, or sitting when I was in the dock. I like to think I built up quite a good relationship with them. They were decent people and I always tried to have a laugh and a joke with them. On one occasion one of them said to me, 'I hope the jury are listening to this,' after a piece of evidence that was particularly damaging to the Crown's case. Another time he said: 'Why is this even here?' He seemed more annoyed than me.

I got to know some of the media guys who covered the trial for its duration. I found *The Sun* and STV were balanced and pretty fair throughout. It was a change from the coverage I had to endure in the wake of the administration. It's telling that the journalists who had been most negative to me over the years were those I'd never met face to face.

Some faces in the public gallery I got to recognise because they came every day. Many were Rangers fans and I ended up talking to some of them. It was interesting to get their opinions, which Paul Kavanagh solicited because we used them as a gauge to sense how the jury might be thinking. After a couple of weeks of the trial, they all thought the verdict would be 'not proven'. That gave me a little bit of confidence. A lot of them ended up being quite friendly to me. I appreciated that there were genuine Rangers fans who wanted to know what happened to their club. It was encouraging that those who had heard the different versions of events were friendly to me. A few Celtic fans were there too, obviously desperate to hear of the shambolic state of their most bitter rivals.

During the trial I sensed the tide of public opinion was starting to turn. Because I had been trying to live as normal a life as possible by going out for dinner and going for runs, as the weeks progressed I started to get recognised even more than normal. Perhaps it was because people had been seeing my face again on TV and in newspapers. Many didn't seem to think I should be in the dock – or others should have been joining me there at least. Some well-wishers shook my hand, wanting their picture taken. I guessed they were Celtic fans.

On one occasion, early on, I was out walking in Glasgow when some Rangers fans shouted abuse. I tried to ignore it and walked on, but just then there was more shouting. A group of Celtic fans had rallied to my defence. As I walked on I could hear them having a go at each other. Only in Glasgow.

The day after the prosecution case concluded, Lady Stacey broke any tension by mistakenly asking Findlay: 'I understand you are closing the Crown case?'

To laughs, he replied: 'I wish I could close the Crown case.'

Findlay then announced to the court that the defence would not be calling any witnesses 'in light of the evidence led thus far'. Lady Stacey told the jury that the prosecution summing up would begin the following day, followed by Donald Findlay a day later. There would be a break for the weekend before she gave her directions and the jury would then retire to consider their verdict.

In his two-hour summing up, Alex Prentice tried to claim that I did not have authority over the funds used in the takeover, and that if Murray had known the true position, the group would not have sold the shares. It was desperate stuff.

'If we accept the evidence, we can accept Mr Whyte knew this was never going to run and took steps to conceal it,' Prentice said. It was simply not the case.

He said the trial was not a public inquiry into the corporate governance of Rangers and there was 'no doubt there were troubling times for the club' but that it had been working within its limits.

On the second charge, he claimed the use of Ticketus money amounted to financial assistance. Prentice said the case was 'relatively simple' and seemed to boil down his argument to one small section of the indictment – whether the share purchase agreement reference to funds from 'its own and third party resources on an unconditional basis' constituted a fraud.

Prentice questioned the insertion of 'unconditional'. He said: 'Why put the word "unconditional" in, what's being achieved here? The Crown say none of it, not a penny of it, was Mr Whyte's, not a penny of it, and all of it was conditional on a number of things occurring before it could be paid.'

The following day, Donald Findlay told the jury I was 'manifestly' not guilty of a crime.

He pounced on the selective nature of Prentice's argument – that he had focused on a single sentence out of 400,000 pages of documents that made up the evidence.

'A recurrent theme of what I will say to you is that the Crown approach is wrong, unfair, unjustified and unjustifiable,' Findlay said. 'They are asking you to take 10 words from the indictment and [arguing] that, if you look at those words, Mr Whyte is guilty.

'The Crown are asking you to be selective in the most selective way imaginable. That is just wrong, that is just unfair.'

Findlay said: 'From the moment [it was] insisted that [the words] 'third-party resources' [were] put into the share purchase agreement, Murray was under notice. You now know that that money is subject to some form of condition, because it has to be. Third-party funding, by its very nature, cannot be unconditional. When those words were put into the agreement, what did Murray's advisers do about it? Absolutely nothing. Why not? Because what mattered was getting the deal over the line. David was let down by those advisers. 'Third-party resources' was an alarm ringing and nobody bothered.'

Findlay tore into the credibility of the Crown witnesses.

'You have seen witness after witness come into court

not wanting to take responsibility and seeking to absolve themselves for anything that happened,' he said. 'It is the playground mentality – it wisnae me. That is the attitude of so many witnesses in this case.'

He said both Murray and I had been 'ill served' by our advisers at the time. In particular, he said Murray had made two 'catastrophic mistakes' following the 2008 financial crisis, which were to entrust the running of the club to people who 'didn't have a clue what they were doing' and leaving everything to his advisers, who 'let him down very badly'.

Findlay said there had been 'buck passing, back protecting and blind eye turning' during the trial. 'What we have to do is sweep all that away and look at it in its context and in the real world,' he said.

No crime, he said, had been committed in the takeover.

By the time I came along, he said, Rangers were in decline.

'The playing squad were declining, the glory days were behind them, hard times were ahead and those running the club didn't know what to do,' he said. 'Murray could no longer bankroll Rangers, there was no more money from Rangers or the bank. Mr Whyte comes along with a plan and thereafter Sir David Murray's advisers are interested in "have you got the money? Have you got the money?"

'The question being asked is money, money, money, week after week, month after month. What was the question they didn't pursue to any extent at all? "Where is it coming from?" Because if that was the question that mattered, surely that was the question you would have expected your lawyer to ask on your behalf.

'They were not interested in where the money came from and we know this absolutely categorically.'

Findlay told the jurors 'the deal was more important than the detail', and reminded them that those advisers spent 'not a single, solitary penny' checking my background or the fine detail.

Referring to me, he said: 'Before this trial started, beyond this court and elsewhere, there have been attempts to portray Craig Whyte as a pantomime villain, the person responsible, so he must take the whole blame. Aided and abetted by the Crown approach, people are now trying to make him the fall guy and that's what this is about, he is being made to be the fall guy. But that is far from the truth.'

He urged the jury: 'You have to look at the whole evidence in this case.'

He pointed out there had been 'no loss' to Murray in the buyout. He spoke of the share purchase agreement and stated the document made reference to 'third party resources'.

He went on: 'What did Murray's advisers do about it? Absolutely nothing. Why not? It is because what mattered was getting the deal over the finishing line.'

Instead, he said, the Murray team had been 'more focused' on securing a sale.

As an example, he highlighted the email written by Mike McGill to David Horne, stating that 'the useless twits don't have the funds'.

'Yet despite that attitude,' continued Findlay, 'they pushed on with the deal.

'Ladies and gentlemen that tells you all you need to know. They didn't care. They just didn't care. The deal was all that mattered.'

On the issue of Ticketus, he said it knew that the funds would be used towards the acquisition of Rangers and any element of secrecy came from the firm itself. He added: 'Nothing, absolutely nothing was held from Ticketus. Ticketus knew from the word go.'

When Lady Stacey began her directions to the jury, she

called for 'cool heads' and urged them to take a 'good, hard look at what has been put before you'. She was the fourth judge I had appeared in front of since this whole saga began and I had considered them all fair.

She picked up on Findlay's earlier comments about me being the pantomime villain and said: 'Now I don't know if you ever read or saw any report to that effect. But if you did, put it out of your minds, please. Please do not be swayed by emotional consideration or any prejudices.'

Ultimately, though, she told the jury the onus was on the prosecution to prove its case. 'Craig Whyte doesn't need to prove his innocence,' she said. 'You must not draw an adverse inference against Mr Whyte because he did not give evidence.'

The jury then retired to deliberate. My fate was in their hands.

For the first time in this whole process, I felt nervous.

# TWENTY-FOUR

AS I WAS sitting on the sofa in my little room, reading a book on my Kindle, in walked Donald Findlay.

'Just to let you know,' he said, 'I've spoken to the judge and the clerk and no matter what, you're getting out today.'

On one hand that was a relief. Even if I was found guilty, I wasn't going to be sent to prison today. It was June 6. Sentencing wouldn't be for a month. I would have some time to prepare. The flipside to this development, however, was it brought home how serious this was. And how it could go either way.

The next time I heard from anyone it was to say the jury had reached a verdict. It had seemed like no time, but two hours had passed. I'd half expected to be waiting a few days for a verdict. Each jury member had a big box of full of files to go through. They must have just gone into the room, had a cup of tea, and came back out again. Everybody had said to me, 'Don't read anything into how long or short a period the jury take before coming out, you just can't tell'. At the back of my mind, though, I couldn't help but read into it. It's quick. It has to be not guilty.

I was pleased. Surely if a jury are going to find someone guilty – after a trial that lasted six weeks, with all that paperwork – they would take a couple of days.

Unless of course they were all raving Rangers fans. So, on second thoughts…

By the time I was back in the dock, the courtroom was busy. All through the trial I'd analysed the jury, or tried to. Who looked sympathetic? Who looked hostile?

There were two guys who sat next to each other. They kept looking over. They have to be Rangers fans, I thought. They don't like me. During the trial, if I bumped into them – it was impossible to avoid bumping into the jurors over that length of period – I'd give them a smile or say 'good morning'. After I smiled at him, one of them seemed okay, but the other one, the older of the two… I just couldn't escape the feeling that he really didn't like me. I had conveyed my thoughts on these two jurors to Donald Findlay, just in case there were things he could say that might influence them.

When they asked the foreman of the jury to 'please stand,' who gets up? The guy who hates me. I'm fucked here, I thought. This is not good.

Have you reached a verdict? They had.

There then was a pause that seemed to last a lifetime.

Charge one? 'Not guilty.'

Charge two? 'Not guilty.'

Relief. Joy. Amazement. Gratitude. All those emotions and so much more. I couldn't believe it.

Lady Stacey addressed me: 'Mr Whyte, please stand up. You've been acquitted, you are free to leave the dock.'

I said thank you to the jury. I thanked the judge. I thanked my legal team.

And that was it. There didn't seem to be any noise in the courtroom, or certainly none that I was aware of. I was probably not focused on that though. Paul Kavanagh took me out of a side door into the room the lawyers had been given.

Donald Findlay told me that just before the verdict was

announced he'd written down a prediction, based on the foreman, in his notepad: 'Guilty.'

I thought about doing a speech outside the court. The media would be there, I was sure. After a bit of deliberating I decided against it, which I think was the right call. I thanked my legal team again and then I went out to brave the media.

The photo everyone used was of me exiting the revolving door out of the High Court laughing. Obviously I was elated at winning the case, but the reason I was laughing was that I'd got stuck in the revolving door with two cops. I was joking that this was probably the worst time for that to happen, when I had all these photographers outside. That was the picture that went everywhere.

I stepped outside into the predictable media scrum. Amid the photographers and reporters was a small bunch of people. Some shouted the odd remark. Clearly these were people that hadn't sat through the full trial.

'I'm just delighted at the outcome,' was all I said.

Sometimes less is more.

I walked towards a waiting car, leaving the rabble behind.

Acres of newsprint and hours of TV time would be given over to so-called experts analysing the merits of the case, the jury's decision and what went wrong at Rangers.

I didn't care. A court had cleared me of any wrong-doing. That was all that mattered.

Where Rangers was concerned, at last I could walk away.

# EPILOGUE

I MIGHT HAVE bought Rangers for a pound, but I didn't take a penny from the club. During the whole sorry saga of Rangers' demise, I am about the only one that can say that. I might not have had to shell out for the Ibrox club, but the cost to me personally since I agreed to take over the debt-ridden mess from David Murray has been incalculable.

I was made bankrupt, lost my businesses and the reputational damage was off the scale.

During the trial, Donald Findlay referred to me as the 'pantomime villain'. However, at times it had felt like I was the most hated man in Scotland. I was, as the High Court jury heard, the fall guy.

I've never known a deal like it – it seemed that everyone I came into contact with tried to shaft me. Many of them succeeded.

Yet, throughout this ordeal, there wasn't anyone I would trade places with. Getting involved with Rangers showed me how much it is an establishment club. And I wasn't part of the establishment.

There was a concerted effort, after the administration, from Murray, the SFA and sections of the popular press to portray me as the bad guy. I had only been there for nine months. I'd bought a bankrupt company for a pound, tried to get it on an even keel in that time, and yet I am portrayed as the villain.

I don't pretend to be an angel. I've cut corners on business deals. I get into messy deals – that's what I do. And that's what Rangers needed. The frustrating thing is, had everyone been pulling together, it was saveable.

I happen to know HMRC said to Duff and Phelps after the administration, 'We really should have done a deal with Craig beforehand, because this is a mess.'

They regretted putting the club into administration.

I had proposed to pay the outstanding tax and I think they realised they had been insane not to do that deal, because they would have got all the money at that time.

Being found not guilty by a jury of my peers was a huge relief. It had been a worrying time for my family and I. But there are no winners in this case.

So how did Rangers end up in this mess – and who is to blame?

To work out why this happened, you have to look at what caused this terrible chain of events. It was the ruinous EBT scheme, which was in operation for 10 years. If the club hadn't gone down that route, it wouldn't have been sold for a pound and it would have been able to get proper funding. The previous board could have battened down the hatches, they could have tried to build up a surplus of cash to deal with the 'big tax case', yet they chose not to do that. They chose to bury their heads in the sand and not deal with these issues. David Murray and the previous board are to blame for the downfall of Rangers.

From the time when Murray took over in 1988 to when he left in 2011 the accumulated losses he incurred for Rangers were somewhere in the region of £130 million. Therefore any suggestion that I had taken over some kind of successful business and ruined it is preposterous.

I was driving the train when it crashed, but I wasn't the one who set it on that disastrous track.

I made mistakes along the way. I should have been upfront about the funding and the dire state the club was in and I deeply regret that.

I prefer to keep my cards close to my chest but on this occasion I should have explained the Ticketus funding. When you compare my acquisition of Rangers to Malcolm Glazer's takeover of Manchester United in 2005 it was far less aggressive or controversial. Rangers were a club mired in debt. Manchester United had been debt free since the 1930s. Glazer's purchase of United was mostly financed by loans secured against the club's assets. The club was saddled with debts of £660 million and interest payments of up to £62 million a year. Some fans were so upset at what was happening they set up a new club called FC United of Manchester.

As it turned out the fans' fears were unfounded. The club raised £500 million from a successful bond issue and by 2010 had paid off the outstanding interest. The club has grown under the Glazer family to become what Forbes magazine rated as the number one sports brand in the world, with a valuation of £3.6 billion.

A lesson there was that however unpalatable a takeover might seem, given the right conditions and with the right business acumen, it could be turned into a success.

My business plan was to make Rangers a profitable business without having to rely on European football. The only time Rangers made a profit under Murray was with Champions League football. That wasn't sustainable but to break even would have been a significant challenge that would have meant reducing the payroll and increasing other types of revenues. Finding other revenue streams wouldn't have been easy but it was what we were looking to do. Ending the retail contract agreed by the previous regime to bring it in-house would have raised several million a year for a start. Developing the area around Ibrox would have helped too. These were things that could and should have been done but our hands were tied.

We could do nothing without first addressing the tax issues. Without resolving that everything else was irrelevant.

Some Rangers fans might think I failed by not putting my own money into the club.

Originally I did think I would raise £5 million to fund the acquisition but once the purchase price dropped to £1 and the two outstanding tax cases became apparent administration was the most likely outcome. In my opinion anyone putting their own money in without the resolution of the tax case had to be mad, because of the real potential it would be lost.

My thinking was that post administration my money could have been used to restart the business. At the point my money would have been safe. As it happened, we never had a chance to do that.

And that is another of my big regrets – not putting the club into administration sooner. I have to live with the consequences of those decisions.

But, not only were there sound reasons for taking the decisions I did, I had no way of predicting that HMRC would liquidate the club over outstanding PAYE tax. Fans should remember that I tried to do a global deal with HMRC for everything that was outstanding, in terms of the small tax and PAYE and working on the assumption we would lose the big tax case. Only then would I have been able to go to the market and raise the money because we'd have clarity going forward.

We had the deal in theory for the big tax case but that couldn't be finalised without knowing what the potential payment plan would be. HMRC also refused to discuss how we would pay the small case liability and any outstanding PAYE arrears. That was highly unusual for HMRC to refuse a six-month repayment plan.

But they did.

And only now do we know why that was.

I was completely in the dark about what was happening behind my back. Other people had agendas and I was powerless to stop them pursuing them.

The negative media attention was like a tsunami. Maybe I should have fought against it more than I did, but it felt impossible to be heard at times. When I did feel like I had some control over what appeared in newspapers, perhaps I was only delaying the inevitable. If I had been more upfront sooner, maybe things would have been different.

There was a snowball effect of negativity. The old board continually spun their lines to the media, which created bad publicity, which hampered the club's ability to do business and dig itself out of the hole it was in.

A confluence of factors caused the club to fold. There was the negativity put out by people like Dave King and Paul Murray; the actions of Duff and Phelps; there was the notice of administration and not getting the 14 days to plan things properly; and there was the poor performance of the team not getting into Europe for only the second time in 20-odd years.

I take responsibility for the part I played in that. I'm not saying I was perfect and I didn't make mistakes – of course I did – but I suffered for it more than anyone, both financially and in terms of my reputation.

I was also battling against a tide of personal attacks. In the aftermath of the verdict, the SFA announced they still intended to pursue me for the fine they imposed.

They banned me for bringing the game into disrepute, but their only evidence was based on newspaper articles. I have since been advised that I have a very good case to sue the SFA. I'm not sure I want to, because it would mean further litigation, but it would be amusing to take them to court.

There was at one point, in 2013, when a legal move was launched by the SFA to get the fine from me. However, we went to court and said we would call Stewart Regan and others as witnesses. Their response was to walk away. They just capitulated and there's nothing they can do to stop me being involved again. If I ever develop a mental illness and buy another football club in Scotland there's nothing the SFA can do to stop me.

They were complete clowns. They had a lot to say about me at the time, but did they say anything about the EBT case?

A club effectively cheated the game for years and no sanctions were taken against any of the individuals responsible.

People might look at the way the new Rangers had to apply for admission to the football league as evidence of punishment, but many of the guys who were there when the problems started are still there – yet still the SFA do nothing about that.

The SFA and the league want a strong Rangers. It is part of their selling point when they are trying to get sponsors that they need to have these two big clubs that are well supported.

Everybody goes on about sporting integrity but at the end of the day the football authorities, if you can call them that, are going to do whatever they can to support the bigger clubs.

I'm not guilty of any crime, and I have nothing to do with the EBT case, but I am banned for life from Scottish football, for inheriting someone else's problems. I find that absolutely outrageous.

Rangers' demise was a complete and utter unmitigated disaster for everybody except Duff and Phelps, and the other insolvency practitioners and law firms.

Companies handling the collapse of Rangers pocketed nearly £20 million in fees while creditors, including thousands of fans, have received just £1.4 million. Insolvency firm BDO have received more than Duff and Phelps, at nearly £10.4 million.

Charles Green didn't do too badly out of it, either.

In each of these cases, people might look and question my judgement. Did Duff and Phelps do anything unlawful? They were after all paid by Rangers on a monthly basis as their client. That no charges have been brought clearly suggest not. However, at the very least I – as I thought their client – whatever the reasons for my misapprehension certainly felt deeply wounded by what happened. The consequences of course for the club were incalculable.

Green was the nominee of the owner. He might argue that he was the owner and therefore could make the switch to a different Sevco but if he really believed that why did he try to deny signing the resignation documents?

Green signed two sets of documents. My associate Aidan Earley had one set. When the police launched their investigation Aidan handed over his copies. Green's fingerprints were found on the letters. Aidan asked DS Robertson how we would get the letters back in case we wanted to sue Green. Robertson told Aidan he would be a witness in any civil case against Green. Charles Green is also on tape confirming he is signing the documents.

It has been a surreal experience. I felt like everyone was conspiring against me. It was almost like I was sub-human. If someone said something, it was okay because it's only Craig Whyte and everybody hates him anyway.

You see people being arrested for sending MPs death threats on social media. I had hundreds of death threats and, to my knowledge, no one has been arrested

It seemed as if I was fair game for anyone. My emails got hacked and I complained to the police. They arrested the person responsible, but he ended up receiving immunity to become a witness against me. Dave King might have been told the leaking of the emails had been authorised by me, which wasn't true, but he bought emails that had been stolen from me, which makes it reset. Did they charge Dave King? No. He was originally going to be a witness against me, too.

Details about King were reported in the aftermath of my case. During legal debate earlier in the trial, which could not be reported until after the conclusion, Donald Findlay QC told the High Court in Glasgow that King had paid for the data.

'What happened at a point in time was an individual known to the Crown hacked into the computer of Craig Whyte and stole material,' Findlay told Lady Stacey. 'It was then used, putting it broadly, for purposes of potential blackmail. The material was subsequently recovered in some way from the thief because of a payment of a significant amount of money by a member of the board of Rangers Football Club, Dave King.'

If I felt at times that everyone was against me, that wasn't helped by the fact that I was in the dock alone, once the charges against the others were dropped. The Crown spent over £1.5 million investigating me, yet didn't see fit to bring cases against anyone else involved.

For the mistakes I made, I was punished severely. For everyone else, it seemed failure was rewarded. Key players involved in the investigation – which was a complete failure from the Crown's point of view – were promoted. The leading police officer was promoted. The Lord Advocate is now a judge.

There were serious conflicts of interest where the Crown

Office was concerned, according to a submission to the Scottish Justice Committee by David Whitehouse, of Duff and Phelps.

As if it wasn't bad enough that the leading police officer was an avid Rangers fan, Whitehouse said that a leading prosecutor was previously married to one of the failed bidders for the club. Whitehouse also claimed senior counsel for the Crown, James Keegan QC, was a known business associate and professional advisor to members and supporters of the Blue Knights who were also failed bidders for the club.

Another serious conflict of interest related to the appointment of experts. The Crown paid thousands of pounds to an accountancy firm to compile a financial report on Rangers. The same firm had a commercial arrangement with another company that was bought by Duff and Phelps. Following the purchase, the commercial arrangement with accountancy firm was terminated, resulting in a loss of business.

Sometimes you almost have to laugh. I'm lucky – I can put things into perspective. I'm healthy and so are my children.

I worried more for my parents, watching their son endure such negativity. They have suffered flak as well, as has practically anyone connected to me.

Only in the last few months have things started to turn around. People are getting that I was not the cause of the problems at Rangers. These issues existed long before I came along. Nobody else has spoken truthfully about what happened to that club.

I don't much care what happens to Rangers now – but I have a lot of sympathy for the Rangers supporters.

I don't follow the story closely, but this is clearly not the Rangers of old. And those fans have suffered more than anyone, and through no fault of their own.

That doesn't take anything away from the fact that Rangers

cheated for years under David Murray and the previous board. I have no love for the tax authorities, but there should be a level playing field in sport and Rangers did not adhere to that by using the EBT scheme to sign players they otherwise would not have been able to bring to the club. That was unfair on the other teams.

That's not the fans' fault, and what worse punishment can there be for a club than to go bankrupt? They lost everything.

I can understand fans of other clubs being aggrieved that the new business retains the titles of the old business. I'm not sure that is a valid claim. But you can't keep kicking the Rangers fans. I just think it's bizarre that a lot of the members of the old board that participated in the cheating and contributed to the problems that went on for years are back there, bold as brass.

When I was considering a quick administration, in and out within a 24-hour period, the pathway was very different. There would have been a 10-point deduction, but Rangers would have continued in the top league; we would still have qualified for Europe that season. Most importantly, it would still have been the same Rangers.

It seemed absurd to me that they had to start at the very bottom tier of Scottish football. The other clubs would not have wanted that to happen. It was completely down to fan power. As I understood it, the fans of other clubs threatened to stop buying season tickets, and I could appreciate their anger. I'm just surprised that the league and the clubs allowed it to happen. It meant a big financial hit for the other clubs, including Celtic.

I'm not sure I get the people still calling for more inquiries, more punishment, the stripping of titles. What would that achieve? Having said that, Rangers is not the same club it once was.

Thankfully, it's not my problem any more. I am back in business and rebuilding my financial position, which is a relief given how devastating that was.

I was the guy that could have saved the club. In some ways, I would like to turn the clock back and have another go. I'd do things a hell of a lot differently.

However, I know one thing for sure – I won't be getting involved with any more football clubs.

The end of this story is the end of my involvement with Rangers. I had hoped it would be different, hoped I could have rebuilt a great Scottish club. It wasn't to be. I was not, could not, be prepared for what came my way. I had thought I was entering a simply business transaction with a loyal fan base who would welcome a soundly run Rangers. I knew it would take time, I knew it would take investment. But I had no time, and I had no chance. So it's time to ask some questions, questions which do not seem to get asked in Scotland.

I am now deemed by the SFA an 'unfit' person to work in Scottish football. Yet the current chairman of the club has 41 criminal convictions, ignored rulings from the Takeover Panel and when he was served with an order regarding contempt of court no one said a word. That court battle ended in March 2019 with the city regulators satisfied he did eventually follow their rules and offered to buy out the rest of the club's shareholders but the case left King with a large legal bill.

When HMRC forced me into administration it was over debts of around £6 million (not allowing for the only recently decided Big Tax Case). Rangers has since then got through a share issue of £23 million, its last accounts revealed soft loans of £17.7 million, it has had to borrow £3 million from a lender of last resort, it has no overdraft facility, and has consistently made multi-million pound losses. And this is deemed a sounder proposition than a prepack administration to move onto a solvent footing?

I am vilified by a Scottish press which gullibly prints every word it is fed from Ibrox and its pressmasters. Not a single difficult question is asked of those who currently run Rangers.

Sectarianism, which I wanted to purge at the club, is once again endemic on its terraces and in its chants. Journalists are threatened, death threats dealt out to writers who dare to examine what happened at Ibrox.

The Scottish Football authorities do nothing, say nothing and hide everything. It was obvious from my own dealings with them that they were hopelessly compromised. Scottish football is a mess; our national team, which once had serious hopes on the international stage languishes. Shouldn't serious questions be asked as to how fit its guardians are for purpose?

And as for the police and Crown Office, I, and others, have been charged, vilified, placed in police custody and yet not a single charge has been proven. Indeed in my own case so pathetic was the prosecution case that we did not even have to lead a defence. How many millions of taxpayers' money have been wasted on the pursuit of nonsensical charges while the really guilty walk away scot-free? Does no one in Scotland think some questions need asked about the Crown Office and Scottish policing. Does their lamentable failure not beg quite a few questions about basic principles of justice in Scotland?

And Sir David Murray, still a Knight of the Realm, despite having run the largest tax evasion scheme in Scottish history, still welcome at the First Minister's residence, despite running his own businesses and one of Scotland's largest sporting institutions into the ground.

This isn't just my story. I have told it because those in

Scotland who should seek the truth are only interested in peddling glib and short-term falsehoods. I can pick myself up and walk away. I can rebuild my business career as I am doing. But this is a story for all Scots of how their country is run, how its press works, who its heroes are.

In trying to give answers I hope I have given many pause to ask some much bigger questions.